Further Travels

IN MY

Mid Eighties

By

Dermot Hope-Simpson.

**An Account of Nine Travels Abroad
During the year of 2016**

authorHOUSE

AuthorHouse™ UK
1663 Liberty Drive
Bloomington, IN 47403 USA
www.authorhouse.co.uk
Phone: 0800.197.4150

Published by AuthorHouse 05/05/2017

ISBN: 978-1-5246-3438-4 (sc)
ISBN: 978-1-5246-3439-1 (e)

Print information available on the last page.

Any people depicted in stock imagery provided by Thinkstock are models,
and such images are being used for illustrative purposes only.
Certain stock imagery © Thinkstock.

This book is printed on acid-free paper.

Contents

This book is dedicated to my Great grand daughter,
Florence

Introduction.

This book gives a further nine journeys I have made since the publication of Travels in My Eighties. I would stress that I have written about the countries as I found them at the time when I was there. In some of these countries there have been considerable recent events which have changed the whole situation. Since I visited. It was not long after my visit to Kurdistan that the so called Islamic State made its appearance there and the country can no longer be visited by the tourist. The Yezidis, now normally spelt Yazidis in our press, have suffered the most for many of these innocent civilians have been brutally murdered, and I also do not know what has happened to some of the Christian communities that I visited and who had been recovering, with the help of the Kurdish Muslim government, from the ravages of Sadaam Hussein. The Kurds themselves who have valiantly resisted ISIL have also, once again, found themselves in conflict with the Turkish authorities after a period when problems there appeared to be being resolved. It seems at the time of writing that famine conditions may be hitting Ethiopia after the failure of the rains. Algeria appears less settled and one can only hope that no real uprising will happen. Even Morocco gives cause for some uncertainty, while Tunisia, which I have often visited, but not since I started writing, has suffered under terrorist attacks. The situation in Syria and Libya seems to go from bad to worse, and when I think of the lovely people I have met and talked to in these and other countries I almost despair for if they were left alone to get on with their own lives they would be happy and would not have to flee from their homes to other places such as Jordan whose native population is believed to be less than half of the numbers of refugees now living there.

Fortunately there are other interesting countries which still appear safe to visit and I am already planning several visits abroad for next year. I find that these trips help to keep me feeling reasonably young and I am even more convinced that the year of one's birth, however long ago that was, should never deter one from travelling.. I find that with the aid of a good travel agent reasonable comfort can be assured. I am of an age I prefer to get someone else to make the arrangements for me rather than trusting to the pressing of a few keys on my computer. As a result of this, I also feel that should something go wrong there are people who will sort out the problem for me.

I am quite often asked whether I prefer to go on a tour or to take a tailor made holiday. I am happy with a tour if it is fairly small for I find that my fellow travellers tend to have similar interests to me, or they would not be on that particular tour and there are always people to talk to.. However quite often the places I wish to visit do not have any tours going there in which case a good English speaking driver, or guide, can show me what I want to see and I am able to spend more time in the places that really interest me. It is easier to change the original itinerary and there is more time to talk to the locals. So there are advantages and disadvantages in both forms of travel. The important thing is to travel to somewhere that interests you and to enjoy every experience you will meet whether planned or accidental.

The author in Myanmar (Burma).

Chapter 1

Myanmar (Burma): A Land of Pagodas.

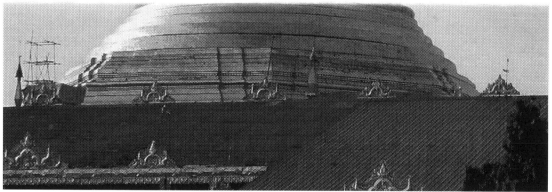

Stupa of the Shwedagon Pagoda.

My first trip in 2013 was to Myanmar, or Burma as it used to be called. I had always wanted to visit this country since several people I knew had fought there during the Second World War, and all of them had said how beautiful it was. However the opportunity had never arisen since for many years it was an enclosed country under a military dictatorship and that remarkable lady, Aung San Suu Kyi was held under house arrest despite having scored a remarkable success in the last General Election held, many years earlier. Apart from anything else she had attended the same college at Oxford as my wife, Jacynth, though not at the same time, and we had both determined that even if we could get in, we would not go there until such time as she was released. Now the military had eased their grip, 'The Lady', as she is usually called there, was not only free but taking a major part in the parliament whose powers were rapidly increasing and tourists were once more welcomed and able to travel round most of the country. I determined to take my chance of a visit before it was either flooded with tourists or the military once again established their rule.

I travelled out by Malaysian Airlines. This was itself an experience for the plane proved to be the largest in which I had ever travelled. It was a two stories high plane and my seat number was 663 despite which there were still many rows behind me. Although I was, as usual, travelling in economy class the service was excellent and the food of a high standard. Indeed it was almost up to Turkish Airlines standard which is the best, by a long way, I had ever previously encountered in any airline. I had asked for an aisle seat when booking in at Heathrow and was surprised when booking in at Yangon (Rangoon) for my return I was surprised, and impressed, to be told even before I had asked "Oh yes. We have you down here as preferring an aisle seat". Another surprise on the return journey was when having breakfast to hear the words," Would you like some more coffee, Mr. Hope-Simpson?" This was certainly the first time I had ever been addressed by my personal name by a member of the cabin staff on any flight.

The only slight hitch was when I had to change planes at Kuala Lumpur on the outer journey' We had been called into the departure lounge for the flight to Yangon (Rangoon) when there was an announcement that there was a technical problem and there would be a delay. We could see our plane and there was no sign of anyone dealing with any technical problem. The only person visible was a man sitting in front of the plane on a little folding chair who occasionally stood up and walked to the front wheel where he kicked the tyre before returning to his seat. After an hour we suddenly saw people walking down the covered way into the plane some of whom went into the pilots' cabin. We were then immediately called to board. The general feeling among the few English there was that the technical problem had been the pilot oversleeping rather than any mechanical failure.

On arrival at Yangon I was quickly through immigration, collected my baggage which was already waiting and found my guide, named Win and his driver named Min. On the way to the Yuzana Garden Hotel we stopped at an exchange where I changed 200 US dollars into the local currency. I had been warned before leaving home that only US dollars would be exchanged and then only if they were in pristine condition and that any notes which were marked in any way, or had the slightest tear or were crumpled would be rejected. Luckily mine all passed scrutiny, though I later met a fellow traveller who has had some of his money rejected.

This currency was to last me for the whole of my trip despite the fact that I had to pay for all of my meals except breakfast. However I was able to pay for a few meals in dollars. Food proved to be very cheap as a rule, many full meals including a large bottle of Myanmar beer costing less than four pounds Sterling. The food was usually very good.

My guide dealt with my booking in while I was given a welcome fruit juice drink, which I found happened at every hotel. My room proved to be a luxurious suite, so I lay down for a siesta, as suggested by Win who said he would call for me at 4pm. However I had hardly lain down when I heard the noise of running water and when I went to investigate in the bathroom I found water pouring through the ceiling onto the floor. The rest of my siesta was interrupted by loud banging from above while a workman tried, eventually successfully, to cure the problem.

I was then taken to see the Shwedagon Pagoda which is generally considered the most holy site in Myanmar.

In the Shwedagon.   *Seated Buddha in the Shwedagon.*

I had never before visited a Buddhist country and had not known what to expect. All shoes and socks had to be removed before entering any sacred precinct. This one was huge. At the centre was an immense golden stupa, pictured at the start of the chapter, which in turn was surrounded by a large number of other buildings. The stupas, of which I was to see a great number during my visit, were usually solid, bell shaped and did not have any entrance. In any important Pagoda or monastery the Stupa would be surrounded by other buildings and rooms. Many of these were called temples and contained holy objects where people would go and worship. Win and I spent at least two hours visiting this particular Pagoda. It was very full of visitors, though the majority of them were obviously Burmese. During my whole trip to Myanmar, I met very few British, though there were a number of Australian, American and, particularly French among the visitors. There were a large number of monks visiting, clearly visible with their shaven heads and deep red robes. A number of the visiting monks were from Thailand and they wore a brighter shade of red. Several of the statues of Buddha were uncoloured and had small fountains or water supplies by them. If you washed these statues it was apparently a way of washing away your own sins and many of the pilgrims were performing this ritual. When we left the Pagoda Win took me to an open air restaurant where I had an excellent meal.

Shwedagon Pagoda

Pilgrims worshiping in temple at Shwedagon.

Washing Buddha at Shwedagon

Visiting monks at Shwedagon.

The next day we were to leave Yangon for one night to visit a place called 'The Golden Rock' which was on the top of a mountain several hours drive away. I was warned to take my night things in my rucksack since we would have to leave the car and my suitcase at the base of the mountain where we would transfer to a truck which would take us up the very rough, narrow, winding road to the village at the top of the mountain. My itinerary also warned me that we would have to leave the truck well below the village and that I would have to be carried in a palanquin for the rest of the journey.

The drive to the base was over very flat land growing many different sorts of crops, including rice and sweet potatoes. The standard of the roads outside Yangon was mainly good and we had to pay a toll to drive on any 'Highway' which was any road with a metalled surface. Everywhere we drove the landscape was dotted with pagodas.

One peculiarity was that though driving was on the right, it had changed from the left at the end of British rule in 1948, 99% of four wheeled vehicles, old and new were still right hand drive. We also found that once we had left Yangon the majority of the traffic was made up by mopeds which were forbidden in most areas of Yangon itself. A recent law imposing crash helmets on riders of these vehicles was still largely ignored in some parts of the country though in others it was applied more strictly. Bicycles with sidecars were still to be seen and it was not uncommon to find an elderly man pedalling along with his wife piled high with shopping by his side.

When we reached the village at the base of the mountain Min disappeared with the car and Win negotiated for our journey in a truck while I relaxed over lunch in another open air restaurant Win's negotiations were successful for he managed to obtain seats in the front by the driver in one of the very crowded trucks.

The drive up proved to be every bit as steep and twisty as I had expected. After about half an hour we had to stop because the rest of the way, another half hour's drive, was only one way and we had to wait for other traffic to come down and there was a waiting area for quite a number of trucks. Communication was by controllers at the top and bottom to allow traffic to move when the way was clear. When we reached a settlement near the top we found that a new road allowed the trucks to drive right up to the top so there was no need for a palanquin, though I was offered, but refused, one for the quarter mile level walk to my hotel. On the way there we had to enter an office to purchase labels to attach to ourselves before we would be allowed to enter the actual religious area in which the Golden Rock was situated.

A truck up the mountain.   *Entrance to the Golden Rock site.*

My hotel, when we reached it, proved to be clean but otherwise one of the most basic hotels in which I have ever stayed. There were a couple of hooks on the wall on which to hang one's clothes and I had to walk through the shower tray to reach the loo.

The Golden Rock religious complex was very large and it was quite a walk, barefooted, from the entrance to the rock itself. This sixty ton boulder is perched very precariously on the side of the hill, held in position, according to superstition, by one hair of the Buddha. It certainly seems extraordinary that it remains in position despite the frequent earthquakes.

I was very disappointed when I arrived at the rock for it was swathed in cloth and scaffolding for repairs were being done to the gold covering which had been wearing out due to weather conditions. The golden covering was, as in so many monasteries and pagodas of real gold leaf and not just painted that colour.

The Golden Rock as normally seen.

The Golden Rock as I saw it.

Despite this disappointment the large religious area around it was itself worth the visit and full of pilgrims, though few western tourists. I was very amused by one of the novice monks, who start as young as the age of two, who was chasing a friend of his with a toy pistol. Unfortunately when I tried to photo this the pistol immediately disappeared inside his robes and he stood formally, looking rather sulky, beside his friend to have his photograph taken.

Novice Monks at the Golden Rock.

Statues of kings at a temple at the Golden Rock.

The time to be there was evidently at the sunset, or sunrise, both of which must have been spectacular with the rock unclothed, and even very fine at the time we saw it. After viewing the sunset we repaired to a Chinese restaurant for a large and excellent meal which cost us the equivalent of less than three and a half U.S. dollars each including drinks and tips.

On our journey down the next day Win once again managed to find us seats beside the driver. I had not realised on the trip up quite how steep the road was and driving downhill round the very sharp bends had me praying that the brakes on the very ancient truck had been kept in good condition.

We eventually reached the bottom in safety and in our own car set off on our return journey to Yangon. We took a different route than that we had travelled on our outward journey. For much of the time we seemed to be driving in an area which had not changed for hundreds of years, with bullocks pulling carts, wooden houses built on stilts with walls of woven bamboo and thatched with palm leaves, workers in the fields ploughing with wooden ploughs pulled by oxen or horses and peasants planting rice by hand.

Our first stop was to see a rubber plantation where everything was being done by hand or hand worked machinery. The young son of the owner was looking very thoughtful and as though he would deal with matters in a much more up to date way when he had grown up and taken over the plantation.

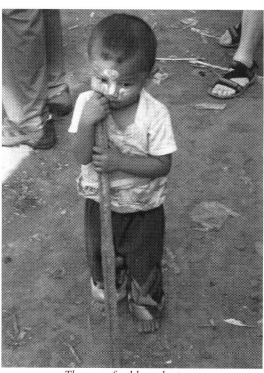

Tappng rubber from tree.   *The son of rubber planter.*

Our next stop was on the banks of a tributary of the Ayeyarwady river as it is now called, its name having been changed from Irrawaddy after the British had left. Here there were half a dozen stalls set up selling dried and salted fish. This was a surprisingly popular tiny market with the locals for a large number of them had come either by boat or by road to buy the produce. Several so called buses arrived while we transportation I was to encounter in several parts of the country though I never plucked up the courage to try the local bus for myself, and certainly health and safety and transport laws would not allow such rolling stock to be used in this country. I resisted all efforts to sell me the produce before entering my car again to be driven to our next stop, the little town of Bago which has a large number of very interesting buildings to be visited.

Rolling rubber into sheets.

Fish market.

Local bus.

The first visit we made was to the Shwemawdaw Paya which with a height of 376 ft is supposed to be the tallest Stupa in the world and is said to house two hairs and two teeth of the Buddha. This building has collapsed and been rebuilt many times over hundreds of years, the most recent being as the result of a huge earthquake in 1930. We also visited the Shwethalyaung Reclining Buddha which was at one time completely lost and covered by dense jungle growth. This is supposed to be the oldest reclining Buddha in Myanmar and at 180 ft long is also one of the largest.

Shwemawdaw Paya , Bago   *Shwethalyaung Reclining Buddha, Bago.*

These are by no means the only artefacts of interest in Bago. We also saw four 100 ft high, the tallest in Myanmar, Buddhas seated back to back and visited the recently restored Golden Palace. How so much gold is used in such a poor country is remarkable. On reaching Yangon we also visited the beautifully maintained Commonwealth War Cemetery.

The Golden Palace, Bag.

In the Commonwealth War Cemetery

The next morning required a very early start and we were at the domestic airport at 5 am. The hotel had provided me with a packed breakfast which, when I opened it, proved to consist of a banana, two slices of white bread and a little pat of butter and a tiny pot of jam. However it had not provided any cutlery with which to spread the butter and jam.

The air terminal itself was very primitive.. There were several flights to Bagan, my destination, and no electric signs at all. When a flight was called a man would appear with a board and a chalk sign proclaiming the destination and flight number. We had each been provided with a coloured sticker to put on our clothing so I kept an eye on other people with the same sticker and followed them when they went .My flight was by Bagan Air, though the plane when we boarded it had the name of another airway on it. It was a very ancient propeller flown plane but delivered us safely after a three quarter of an hour flight. Here we walked to the terminal and waited for our luggage which was unloaded and carried by hand from the plane and only given over to the owner on the production of an identity tag.

My new guide, called Nine, was waiting for me with his car and driver and took me first to my hotel to deposit my luggage, for my room was not yet ready, before driving me to see a local market.. This, like several other markets I was to visit during my trip, had not yet made any concessions to the tourists and so was much more interesting being entirely devoted to local needs.

Local market in Bagan.   *The sticks on the stall were to make anti sunburn paste.*

We next set about visiting a few of the 3,200 pagodas situated in or about Bagan. The majority of these Pagodas were built out of brick or stone and were, to my mind, more attractive than the gilded buildings. However the first of our visits was to one which was gilded and was also one of the largest of the religious buildings in the area. The importance of this building is seen from the huge marble Dragon guarding its entrance, as well as the very large gold covered complex I was particularly amused at the sight of a very young novice monk sitting on a wall devouring a very large slice of water melon which some pilgrim had obviously given him and was in haste to finish before mid day after which the monks are not allowed to eat until the next morning.

Pagoda entrance. Bagan.   *Pagoda Temple and Stupa. Bagan.*

Novice Monk.   *Pagoda Temple. Basgan.*

We then had an excellent lunch in an open air restaurant before returning to the hotel for a rest. The hotel was situated in a lovely garden with some magnificent Banyan trees which gave welcome shade to the restaurant at meal times. One of the main buildings in the hotel had a large plaque on it reading. *"THIS BUILDING WAS SPECIALLY CONSTRUCTED IN 1922 TO HOUSE H.R.H. THE PRINCE OF WALES (WHO LATER BECAME KING EDWARD VIII) WHEN HE VISITED BAGAN."*

After my siesta I was collected and taken to see a little factory which specialised in the making of lacquer. This proved to be a remarkable process. I had always assumed that the lacquer vases I had seen were ceramic pots. However here the vases were first woven with bamboo. Then the bamboo vase was coated with a thick black gooey substance before being taken down to a cold dark cellar for at least six weeks for the black to dry out. When it was considered ready it was brought out again and the black was smoothed with some abrasive. Then some of the surface was etched with a sharp tool and the etched area covered with a coloured dye. After another period in the cellar the vase was brought out again and the coloured dye was washed off the surface but left in the etched area. Then another area was etched and a different colour applied. The whole process was repeated again and again until the final colours and pattern had been completed. It was reckoned that a small vase might take six months from start to finish.

I was then driven to the quayside of the Ayeyarwady river where my guide and I boarded one of the many boats assembled there. Most of the boats had large groups on them but my boat, though the same size as all the others only had me, my guide and the boatman on it. We went some distance upstream past several pagodas and a small boat building area when our little engine was turned off and we relied on the current to take us downstream again. My guide told me that on some of the boats the passengers were told that their engine had broken down. Indeed we actually saw one boat where the boatman was unable to restart his engine at the correct time and he had to be taken in tow. Our timing was excellent for we watched a wonderful sunset before coming in to land.

Boatbuilding on the Ayeyarwady river.   *Sunset over the river.*

I took dinner, another excellent meal, in the open air restaurant under a Banyan tree, at the hotel. We were entertained there by a man who played a musical percussion instrument which was unknown to me and a girl who sang to his music and then gave a remarkably skilful string puppet show by herself. She stood overlooking the stage and could be seen working the puppets one at a time unlike the other puppet has been acted. But the skill with which she worked was extraordinary. One puppet was a footballer who not only kicked the ball around but back kicked it up to his head and bounced it several times there.

While there I shared a drink with a British couple, two of the very few British I was to meet in the country, whose son had been taught by an old friend of mine.

Bagan hotel with Banyan tree   *Bagan music and puppets.*

The next morning was devoted to visiting several of what I was told were the best temples in Bagan, the tallest, the oldest and the most beautiful. The whole area was so covered with these buildings that I was quite unable to remember their various names. Several of them had stalls outside selling, mainly, religious objects. Outside one monastery was a stall selling pictures painted in coloured sand with the artist busy at work. I was very attracted to one picture but as it was rather larger than I wanted I decided to think about it while I went around the building. Then inside the complex I found another similar stall with an equally attractive painting so I bought that instead. When we left I wondered if I should explain to the artist my reason for buying another picture, but my guide said "You don't need to feel guilty. The stall you bought your picture from was run by his sister and all the pictures she was selling were by him."

Pagodas in Bagan.

All the temples had statues of the Buddha inside them and some of them had frescos on the walls, though many of these were very faded.

Buddhas in Bagan.

After lunch I was taken back to the hotel for the usual siesta, but I decided instead to walk to the Archaeological museum which was just outside the entrance of my hotel. It proved to be a 19th Century building which housed many treasures from old Bagan which had been rescued from decaying pagodas as well as modern models and drawings to show what the city must have been like in the past.

Soon after my return to the hotel my guide collected me again and we visited the only Mon Pagoda left in Myanmar. The Mon were one of the oldest peoples to inhabit Myanmar but were gradually overcome and assimilated by other tribes. This particular temple was distinguished inside by an immense seated gold covered Buddha and what is described by the Guinness Book of Records as the largest collecting bowl for alms in the world. One has to climb a ladder to be able to pay one's gift.

Buddha uin Bagan. · *Fresco in Bagan*

Begging bowl in Bagan Mosque. · *Seated gold Buddah.*

Nine then took me on my final trip to see the sunset over Bagan. He explained to me that he was not taking me to the usual view point which became rather crowded and instead he took me to another pagoda a little distance away. To get to the roof I had to enter a very narrow archway into an even narrower corridor and climb up some very tall steep steps under an extremely low roof. Nine asked me if I thought I could manage them. Looking through the archway I could see daylight at the top of some twenty of these steps, so I said I thought I could manage them, calculating that I could just about get down by sitting on each step in turn. However on reaching the apparent top it was, in fact, a very narrow right hand turn before another equally difficult and tall flight and the light I had seen was coming down from the real top. However I eventually made it.

From the top there was a marvellous view out over a large number of pagodas and I could see several coach loads of other tourists climbing up another pagoda, about half a mile away, on an open stairway. There was no one else on the roof of my pagoda except for my guide and driver. The pagodas glowed brightly under the setting sun until, unfortunately, it disappeared under some clouds near the horizon and the actual sunset itself was a nothing like as fine as that of the previous evening. When it came to the time to descend Nine insisted I follow him down backwards with him leading me and placing my feet in turn on each step in turn I still think this way of doing things was more difficult than the sitting down one step at a time would have been.

When we did eventually reach the bottom he congratulated me and said that the last couple he had taken there, who were a lot younger than me, had taken one look at the steps and refused to climb them so he had had to take them to the usual tourist viewing point.

Sunset over Bagan.   *Usual tourist viewpoint.*

The next morning we left for the airport at 6:30. On arrival we were told that there would be a delay of an hour because thick fog at Yangon had meant that no planes there were able to take off, and our plane was one of these. After some two hours we were sent to a departure lounge, through a door labelled "Baggage and Cargo." It was over another hour before six or seven planes landed in quick succession. We watched large piles of luggage being pushed around haphazardly on hand trolleys before we were suddenly ordered to walk out to a plane parked near the terminal. Here we had to wait while some of the new arrivals dismounted from the plane. As soon as the final passenger left the steps we were rushed up into the aircraft, where we took the first seats available, the doors were slammed shut and we took off again only seven minutes after the last passenger had left. It was the quickest turnaround I had ever encountered. Somehow or other all our luggage had been loaded in that time, for no one appeared to be missing their cases when we landed at Mandalay after a flight of only twenty minutes.

When we arrived I found, rather to my surprise, my new guide and driver waiting for me The drive to the city of Mandalay took over an hour, for the airport had been built a considerable distance away so that it could also serve a new city which was to be built at a similar distance in the opposite direction. We entered a narrow very badly surfaced street and stopped so that I could see a shop where stone carvings were being made. The next visit was to a nearby temple where visitors could buy gold leaf to put on a seated Buddha. This statue was installed in 1910 without any gold covering. It is now reckoned that the gold on the image weighs over three tons and that on the canopy above weighs even more.

Stone carving in Mandalay.   *Buddha with gold leaf in Mandalay.*

We then stopped at a restaurant where a huge lunch and beer cost me 4,500 Kyats which is about 3.5 U.S. dollars. Altogether the food in Myanmar so far had proved very cheap. I was then taken to the Mandalay Swan Hotel and ensconced in a very luxurious room and bathroom, where I had the normal siesta before my guide appeared and took me off for

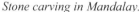

We started with a visit to a very crowded street market and which appeared very dangerous due to the number of mopeds weaving around among the pedestrians. Indeed Mandalay seemed to have thousands of these vehicles, with about half of the riders wearing crash helmets. I was told, again, that there had been a recent law passed making the wearing of these helmets by moped drivers compulsory, but that the law was not yet being rigorously enforced. While in Yangon itself mopeds were not allowed, here they seemed to have become far and away the commonest form of transport, but despite the wild driving I never saw a moped driver involved in any accident. In the market I watched the correct type of wood being ground into a moist paste which was then applied to the face to prevent sunburn. This was very common throughout the country and can be seen clearly on the faces of many people shown in my photographs. Some of this paste was painted on my face at this time but I cannot say that it made any difference to me in the feel of the sun's rays.

We then went to see a wooden monastery. The majority of the religious buildings had at one time been made of wood but over the years most of them had been replaced by stone or brick buildings and very few of the wooden ones now remained. When we arrived a service was taking place and we could hear lovely chanting from the monks. When the service was finished we were able to see the inside for only a very short time before the monastery was shut since there was no electricity in the building. Some restoration was being done and the scaffolding and ladders were made of bamboo. The only stonework visible was the steps and wall leading up to the building, and there were some lovely flowers growing up the wall.

Wooden Monastery in Mandalay.

Flowers on steps wall.

After our return to the hotel I visited a local restaurant for supper of sweet and sour pork with rice and a local desert, the whole excellent meal washed down with some fine Myanmar beer. My only complaint about the meal was that it was far too large for me to manage it all. Once again it was cheap costing only six dollars with the tip included.

The next day started with a visit to a monastery library. On the way we passed a completely naked middle aged lady walking along by the road. No one seemed to be in the least surprised by this sight in a busy city street. The library itself contained a number of rare manuscripts, some written on palm leaf, some on wood and some on parchment. All had to be viewed with the aid of a torch since it was very dark and there was no electricity.

Then we drove to the largest monastery in Mandalay which contains over a thousand monks. Here we were able to see food preparation, cooking, monks washing before their meal and finally queuing up with their bowls for their food to be doled out to them by monks and lay people, some of whom had been responsible for providing the food. Monks rely entirely upon alms with which to buy their food, despite which they do not appear to go short. I was amused to see that some of the young novice monks already had bars of chocolate, presumably given by visitors, in their bowls before they joined the queue. This, at eleven a.m., was ,of course, to be their final meal of the day since no eating was allowed after midday. It was interesting that this was a public spectacle and that there were many visitors and tourists who came to watch and to photograph the proceedings.

We next drove to a large lake, which was crossed by a 1.2 kilometre wooden pedestrian bridge, the worlds longest teak bridge Coloured fishing boats were drawn up at the edge of the lake. There were also a number of stalls, one of which held baskets of live song birds which people would buy and immediately release. This was evidently counted as a good deed. I also bought a small carved stone elephant which claimed to be made of jade. I had strong doubts about this but it was so cheap I bought it and only found later, to my surprise, that it probably really was jade for Mandalay is a centre for that stone.

Monastery kitchen.

Monks queuing for food.

World's longest teak bridge.

Fishing boats by lake.

Before driving to a ferry across the river, a tributary of the Ayeyarwady, we visited a

the manufacturing trades in the country still carry on in the old way without the introduction of modern machinery and I was to see many more fairly primitive factories later on in my trip.

The ferryboat to Inwa was equally old fashioned and the one which was leaving as we arrived looked very overcrowded and if there had been a plimsoll line it would have been well below the water level. Luckily there were not so many people waiting for the next ferry and we completed the five minute journey in comparative comfort and safety. For several centuries Inwa was Burma's old royal capital. It is now a rural backwater of monasteries and Stupas, some of which are still active while others are in ruins, though several are under repair. There do not appear to be any made up roads, and the only transport I saw were a very few mopeds and a large number of horse pulled carts, one of which we took for our exploration of the place. The horse pulling our cart was young and frisky and had obviously not yet completed its training so we had a considerably more active and bumpy ride than the majority of the other carts which seemed to be drawn by much older and more sedate horses. Indeed on several occasions the driver almost lost control of his steed. It all made for an exciting ride.

Ferry across the river, local transport at Inwa.

Our first visit was to one of the buildings under repair with the usual bamboo pole scaffolding around it. This was followed by a drive through fields, with women squatting and working at rice, to a large wooden monastery which had a huge sign outside it saying, in capital letters in Burmese and English "BAGAYA MONASTERY. BAGAYA MONASTERY WAS BUILT IN 1834 A.D DURING THE REIGN OF KING BAGIDAW. BEING BUILT ENTIRELY OF TEAKWOOD, THE MONASTERY HAS 267 GIANT POSTS, THE BIGGEST POST MEASURING 60 FEET HIGH AND 9 FEET IN CIRCUMFERENCE. THE MONASTERY IS A STRUCTURE OF GREAT DIMENSION FOR IT IS 188 FEET IN LENGTH AND 103 FEET IN BREADTH. THE MONASTERY IS A STOREHOUSE OF MYANMAR CURTURAL HERITAGE, REPRESENTING ANCIENT ARCHITECTURE AND SCULPTURE IN SEVERAL ARTISTIC OBJECTS WHICH ARE RARELY FOUND IN THE MONASTERY OF A LATER DATE." This proved to be an interesting visit since there was a school inside, where some young novices and other very young children were being taught by a monk who had evidently set his charges some work to do and was busy reading a newspaper ignoring his pupils, the younger of whom were busy fooling about while not leaving their seats.

Our next visit was to Maha Aungmye Bonzan monastery, built in 1822 as a royal monastery temple, and the largest in Inwa. There was a very impressive entrance with two dragons but quite a large part of the building was closed. A notice announced "No Enter. The danger can be occur by (11.11.2011) Earthquake."

Entrance to Maha Aungmye Bonzan Monastery.

Maha Aungmye Bonzan Monastery.

We finished the trip to Inwa with lunch at an open air restaurant where I was joined by a South African travelling alone. He was trying to get to Yangon but had found that there was not a single spare bed in the city for the next two weeks such is the present shortage of hotels there and did not know what he was going to do next.

On our return, back across the river on an empty ferry, I was taken to see several factories including wood carving, needlework, puppet making and, quite the most interesting, the making of gold leaf from little bits of gold, an operation involving hours of manual beating by heavy hammers.

Needlework.

Gold leaf making.

When we returned to the hotel I found a large marquee had been erected on the lawn between the hotel and the main road and there were ominous sounds of musical instruments being tuned up inside. Someone said that it was a celebration of the Chinese New Year that might well go on all night. However the hotel informed me that it was a new local band and that the music would stop at midnight. Luckily, for my room overlooked the marquee and the noise was tremendous, this proved to be the case and I was able to get a reasonable night's sleep. Since there appeared to be crowds everywhere I decided to eat in the hotel where I had another good meal and I met a pleasant English couple from Bath and found that the husband had been a boy at Plymouth College, but before my time.

Next morning I reached the airport at 6.45 a.m. for the flight to Heho. However nothing is normal about Bagan Airway. I was duly booked in to fly, nonstop according to my ticket, at 8.50, arriving at 9.15. However we took off at 8.30 and landed at 8.50., left the plane and mounted the coach for the Terminal. Then a man rushed up to the coach and said that those who had boarded at Mandalay and were bound for Heho should not have disembarked since this was Bagan and not Heho. So a dozen or so of us climbed back on to the nearly empty plane. The plane then filled up with travellers from Bagan to Heho, including a large French tour. This time we really did go to Heho landing only 15 minutes later than our original schedule.

I was duly met by my new guide who seemed at first to be a young girl but who I later found to be in her mid forties, with a name something like Nino, and our male driver. I later found she was a Christian, my first two guides having been practising Buddhists and the third a Free thinker. We then drove for about two hours over awful roads through lovely European type mountain scenery to the village of Pindaya where we stopped to see the ubiquitous umbrellas being made. This proved to be another fascinating visit, Wood from Mulberry trees is first hammered into a paste and then put into a pan of water where petals from a fruit tree are scattered over it by hand. When dry it is taken out of the pan in a sheet ready to be fitted. Bamboo is then used to make the frame. Everything is done by hand, or hand and foot worked pedals. Red umbrellas are also made for monks.

Umbrella making.

After lunch in another open air restaurant we went on to visit Shwe Oo Min Natural Cave Pagoda, the most extraordinary cave I have ever seen. We parked the car at the bottom of a hill and walked up to where a modern lift took us up to the cave entrance. The cave itself is filled with nearly nine thousand statues, mainly Buddha images, of every size, many of them covered with gold leaf or paint. Two uncovered statues are known as the weeping Buddhas since they sit under a steady drip from stalactites above which makes it impossible to coat them with any artificial coating. Some of the statues are in effect gold covered stupas. There is a legend that on one occasion seven princesses took refuge in the cave during a storm but then found themselves imprisoned by an evil spirit in the shape of a giant spider. However a prince, walking nearby heard them shouting for help and shot the spider dead. There are now statues by the entrance to the caves showing this event.

Lift to cave entrance.

Statue by cave entrance.

Images in cave.

Weeping Buddha in cave.

I was next driven to the Kalaw hill top Villa situated up in the mountains and with attractive gardens and fine views. Before leaving the cave I had been amused to see a large party of, mainly novice, monks who had been visiting climbing into as well as onto the top of a mini bus which was to be their transport back to their monastery.

Transport for monks.

View from Kalaw Hotel.

At the hotel I was to meet again two Americans that I had met before in both Bagan and Mandalay, who like me were doing an individual tour. I gathered they had had, an awful hotel in Mandalay and had not seen nearly as much as me.

The next day when I returned to my room I found that the lock had broken and that I could not open the door. A member of the staff was summoned and finally managed to force a way in. My first visit of the day was to the local market in Kalaw. This proved to be a very large open air affair designed entirely for the locals, consisting mainly of various foods, including many spices, and not for the tourists. In fact the only other tourists I saw during my visit was the same American pair. Many of the locals could be distinguished by their dress as being from different villages.

Kalaw Market.

We then drove back past He Ho airport and on through attractive rural countryside, much of which, including bullock drawn carts, did not appear to have altered for hundreds of years, to the village of Nyaungshwe which is next to the main canal leading to Inle Lake. Here after yet another excellent meal in a lovely open air restaurant my luggage was

25

unloaded into a boat belonging to the local agents so that the only passengers were my guide and myself plus the boatman. This was to be the same transport for my time on the lake so I felt rather smug when I viewed many other boats of the same size, full of passengers. This is one of the most popular areas for tourists to Myanmar, though the number of them was only a trickle compared to most countries. During the trip to my hotel I found that my guide had studied chemistry at university but unable to get a job had worked for a time at an hotel where she had taught herself English before becoming a guide at which job she excelled.

Local Transport.

Lake Inle is truly extraordinary. There are on it quite a number of manmade floating islands, fixed to the floor of the lake by long stakes, and crops are grown on these islands. Some new islands are still being made and I was told that it took fifty years to build each one. The houses are built standing on poles above the surface of the water and there are several such villages there where, of course, the only way to reach a house is by boat. A lot of the local fishermen still propel their boats by oars attached to their legs, though some use ordinary oars and an increasing number of the boats now have outboard motors attached.

A fisherman (Not leg propelled).   *A new floating island in the making.*

On our way to the hotel we visited the "Jumping Cats" monastery built in the lake. It derives its name from the time, until a year or two ago, the monks used to train their cats to jump through hoops. They have now been forbidden to do that so the cats seem to spend most of their time sleeping on mats. Nevertheless it is still a fine and active wooden monastery built, like the ordinary houses on stilts above the surface lake. I had hoped to see the famous floating market, where everything is sold from boats and which used to function once every five days. Unfortunately it has now been closed by the authorities who considered it had grown too large to be safe. The next morning I was woken at 5 o'clock by some loud music from some boats or a local monastery; I never discovered which. I was to visit, the next day, a large market which had grown up on the lakeside near a mosque not far from the site of the old floating market. Despite the fact that the first two stalls we saw were devoted to the tourist the rest of the very large bazaar was entirely devoted to the locals and proved to be the finest that I had visited despite the fact that practically all the people there had had to arrive by boat. One small fascinating thing was the way that different stalls had completely different ways of weighing their products.

Landing place for market.   *Market.*

27

One of the weighing measures at the market.

We spent quite a long time in the market before going to visit the nearby mosque and pagoda of Phaung Daw Oo Paya with its five Buddha images inside. These had been brought to the building in a boat which had sunk in a storm. According to legend four of them had been discovered and rescued but the fifth had mysteriously made its own way to the Pagoda. There are photographs there which show the unadorned Buddhas as they appeared when first installed but they are now covered with so much gold leaf that their original shape is invisible. Once a year they are paraded right round the lake in a highly decorated barge. I resisted the temptation to add yet another piece of gold leaf to any of the images.

The Buddhas as they were when installed   *The Buddhas as they are now.*

After viewing the Pagoda we took to our boat again and the remainder of the day was spent in using this form of transport since everywhere we visited was on the lake as opposed to dry land. Our first visit was to a place weaving silk, cotton and lotus. One of the interesting things was to see the lotus being prepared by hand ready for the weaving.

Preparing the Lotus plant for weaving.

A main street, Lake Inle.

After I had purchased a lotus and silk tie we moved on to a restaurant on its stilts and with an excellent view of the passing boat traffic where I met an Australian who had been one of us who had descended from the plane at the wrong, and unscheduled, stop on the way here. His hotel proved to be on dry land on the lakeside. Our next visit was to a blacksmiths where five men were doing the work that one would do in England and this was followed by a business making cheroots. Once again all the work was being done by hand. All our visits this afternoon were by boat to wooden houses built on sticks into the lake and such machinery as there was manually operated.

We then travelled on to a place making boats where there was no machinery of any sort. Everything was done by hand. Here they had realised that they could make a little money from the tourists for they had for sale a number of toy boats made out of small pieces of leftover wood. The silver workshop we visited next was a family firm which had been run by the same family for three generations. Here the process started with breaking up the ore, by beating it with hammers to extract the raw silver and finished with beautiful handmade jewellery and artefacts.

Boatbuilding.   *Silver making.*

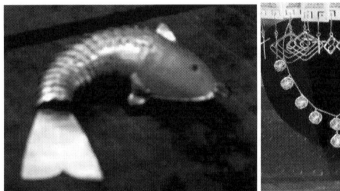

Some of the silver jewellery made here.

Our final visit of the day was to another weaving place, but this was probably the most extraordinary of the lot for it was run entirely by ladies with long necks from a tribe in the north of the country. Here every female baby, when it reaches the age of two has a ring put round its neck, and a new ring is added each year for many years. It makes a most bizarre sight, and I was not surprised to find that there were now only some 60,000 of these people left in the country.

The long necked weavers.

At some point during the day the tops of my feet were becoming very painful and I originally blamed my new sandals for rubbing the skin. It was only when I returned to the hotel that I discovered that it was not their fault but that it was being caused by severe sunburn on the parts of my feet that were not covered by the sandal straps. Luckily I had worn my sun hat every day.

The next morning we left the hotel at about 6.00 in the morning, just as the sun was rising and had a lovely boat trip back across the lake, with only fishing boats visible on the very still water, to where we were met by our car and driver for the journey back to He Ho airport for my flight back to Yangon. On this occasion we flew in a plane actually labelled "Bagan Air" and were served with a small sandwich meal. My guide, Win, was waiting for me and first took me to see the longest reclining Buddha, in the country, over 200 feet long and with lettering inscribed on the soles of the feet, before taking me to see the house of 'The Lady' viewed over the lake which an American swam causing her to be imprisoned for a further length of time.

We then visited what I might describe as a very crowded but very local restaurant where we were squeezed onto a bench with not another foreigner in sight. The meal, however, was excellent and cost practically nothing.

After booking in at the hotel and a siesta we travelled to the centre of the city where we first visited the Sule Paya. This, while not as large as the Shwedagon, is a large and interesting group of buildings occupying the middle of the largest traffic circle in the city

Sule Paya.

Once again there were several temples and pilgrims washing Buddhas though the whole was not nearly as crowded as the Shwedagon. Nearby were several nineteenth century British buildings including the Strand Hotel, similar to the Raffles Hotel in Singapore, which we also visited before travelling to the river and docks which do not appear to have changed very much since the British left.

We also visited Royal Palace of Buddha's Bronze Image at the Botataung Paya, which is believed to have held eight strands of the Buddha's hair for a period of time. During the last war a bomb scored a direct hit. However after the war the Paya was rebuilt in a similar style except for the Stupa which was rebuilt as a hollow structure where were standing many glass showcases holding many ancient relics. There is also a hall holding a large gilded bronze Buddha which had been shipped to London by the British many years earlier but which was returned upon Myanmar gaining its independence.

Botataung Paya   *Washing a Buddha.*

Our final visit of the day was to see the huge Royal Barge on the Royal lake.

The Royal Barge.

The next morning we returned to the airport stopping for a view over the lake to the Shwedagon and then to see two sacred white elephants which are kept in a small room during opening times, but a apparently allowed to roam over a very large area at other times.

The journey home involved a six hour wait changing planes at Kualar Lumpur but there were comfortable arm chairs in one area where I was able to sit and watch the BBC television news programme. The food on the flight was once again excellent and the flight punctual.

Chapter Two

Bulgaria: A Country of Painted Churches.

The Lion Bridge, Sofia.

My next trip of 2013 was to Bulgaria, a country I had just visited with my wife, Jacynth, some ten years before. However then we had stayed for only one week in a village called Bansko so except for several day visits out from there the country was new to me. I flew by British Airways to Sofia. Luckily my alarm clock was set for my Heathrow hotel failed to give me my booked alarm call. The flight started late because one of the hold baggage doors would not shut and they had to call in an engineer to fix it. When I reached Sofia I was met by a girl from the local agents who drove me to my hotel and told me that my guide for the tour, George, would call for me the next morning since he was just finishing off leading a tour that day. She also told me of a good restaurant some ten minutes walk away since my hotel only had a delicatessen where I would get breakfast but which did not serve other meals. I then took a walk to the centre of the city which was not far away. During my walk I visited the Rotunda, or Church of St. George, the oldest preserved building in Sofia, part of it said to be dating from Roman times. It, as well as a small area which is being excavated, is surrounded by large modern buildings. There are some attractive early frescos inside though photography there was forbidden,

The Rotunda or Church of St. George

I did not visit any other buildings at this point but contented myself with looking at the exteriors expecting that George would take me to the best places the next day. I found the centre to be very attractive, most of the buildings being built in the 19th century

That evening I walked across the Lion Bridge, just in front of my hotel and found the restaurant which had been recommended to me .I decided that the recommendation had been very good for the meal was superb. I was later to find that the general standard of Bulgarian cuisine was very high. I had a long chat with a middle aged Japanese lady, sitting on the next table, a teacher who was also travelling on her own but who was more adventurous than me in that she had no guide nor had she prebooked any accommodation or travel.

The next morning was cloudy and it looked like rain, which I was told was forecast. However the clouds soon cleared and it turned into a fine sunny day with perfect temperatures. My guide, George, arrived in his car at the allotted time. He told me that Sofia had had the warmest April since records began with temperatures reaching the upper thirties unlike us in England who had had a very cold April, though now in early June I had left under clear blue skies.

George was to prove an excellent guide who also spoke very good English. I found he was on the committee of the largest body of guides in Bulgaria. He soon found out my interests and took me to a number of places not on the original itinerary which he thought might interest me and indeed they were some of the best places we were to visit.

The first building we visited was the 19th century St Aleksandur Nevski Memorial Cathedral Church. which I had admired from outside the previous afternoon.

Aleksandur Nevsky Memorial Cathedral.

He then proposed a visit to the Rotunda and was surprised to find that I had already visited it the previous day. So we had a long tour round the centre including many places I had not yet seen.

The Russian Church, Sofia   *The Theatre, Sofia.*

We next took the car and drove out to the suburbs to see the Boyana Church with its famous 11th to 16th century frescos. Jacynth and I had hoped to get into this building on our earlier visit but were informed the church was closed for some reason so did not come to Sofia.. George had timed our visit carefully for a less crowded time since it is a tiny church and only a small number of visitors is allowed in together for a limited period with the official guide and at many times of day people have to wait nearly an hour for entry. We were lucky this lunch time and arrived in front of a large group. Just before we entered we were hailed by the previous night's Japanese lady who had recognised me so she joined us for the visit, as did two Italians who had been waiting for a long time. The official guide knew George and allowed him to tell us about the frescos and did not seem to mind when we considerably over ran our time. Despite its small size all the walls and ceiling are covered with hundreds of frescos in very good condition despite their age..

Boyana Church with frescos.

After our visit we stopped for coffee at a local restaurant, together with our Japanese friend to whom we gave a lift back into the centre. On the return journey we stopped so that I could buy a new rubber ferule for my walking stick since the original one had fallen off at some point.

On our return George left me and I spent much of the afternoon on further exploration by myself and spent over an hour in the Archaeological Museum and saw the mosque on my way to visit the Synagogue and then the first covered market in Sofia, which I must admit was not a patch on many of those I had seen in Myanmar and the Middle East.

It was interesting that many of the pedestrian underpasses have Roman remains under them.. I was also surprised to find yellow ceramic tiles used as road coverings in one area. How well they survived the traffic I do not know, but the tiles all seemed to be in good condition.

There was heavy rain during the night and it proved to be an unsettled day weather wise with showers when we were driving and a large storm while we were lunching, but luckily it was dry while we were sightseeing on foot. I was surprised at breakfast by the Japanese lady who had come into the delicatessen to buy some cakes. During our conversation she discovered it was my birthday and dashed back to her hotel to fetch me a present! This proved to be an attractively woven Japanese table mat.

Synagogue, Sofia

George and I were now to drive to Bansko, stopping on the way at the Rila Monastery of The Nativity of the Virgin Mary. both the largest and the most visited monastery in Bulgaria. It is particularly famous for its frescos and while photography was not allowed inside the church itself many of the best paintings were on the exterior walls of the church, protected by a covered walkway. Extensive buildings, including monks living quarters and a museum completely surround the church and the five storey Hrelyo Tower, the oldest building in the complex. We were delayed entering the church and the museum because of a power cut but George employed the time marvellously by explaining to me the meanings of the external frescos many of which were not immediately obvious.

None of the frescos is particularly ancient since they date from the rebuilding of the church in the 1860s after it has been reduced to ashes by a fire, though the original foundation of the monastery appears to have been in the tenth century and the tower dates from that time.

Some frescos from Rila Monastery.

The Rila Monastery

Inside the church there was a fine iconostasis which was interesting in that at the bottom instead of the usual painted flowers it had painted shields, a memory of the war of freedom against the Ottomans. We had lunch of fresh trout at a nearby restaurant before driving on to Bansko where we found our hotel in an excellent position in the centre overlooking gardens.

I had remembered Bansko as a lovely village but shortly after we had returned to England from our earlier visit one of newspaper travel supplements had started with a large headline "Baby Bansko goes for the big time". It then carried on saying it was going to be developed as the largest ski resort in Bulgaria. I also gathered that a large number of new hotels was being built. I was relieved to find out that very little had changed and I could only assume that all the new hotels had been built some way out of the town by new ski lifts which I never found.

After settling in I went for a walk round and visited the church where I had previously heard a lovely choir singing. I had forgotten that, unlike most Orthodox churches it had plenty of seating, I also found the little hotel in a backstreet where Jacynth and I had stayed on our previous visit and was glad to find it little changed.

That evening I dined at the hotel at the suggestion of George who said he had stayed there before and said the food was very good. After an excellent main course with some fine red wine I asked for the menu for desserts. The head waiter held up his hand, smiled, shook his head and said "Surprise". It really was a surprise when it arrived for they had evidently found out it was my eighty fourth birthday, either from my passport or from George. There appeared a sculptured dish in the form of a castle, surmounted with several lit candles, made up of a large number of slices of many different fruits. Unfortunately I had left my camera in my room and so could not take a photograph. It was far too large a dish for me on my own but luckily there was an English girl eating there with her Polish partner so I was able to pass the remains to them. The waiter then brought me some coffee and when I asked for my bill refused to take any payment at all.

View of Pirin Mountains from Bansko.   *Bansko Street.*

The next day started cloudy but it soon became sunny and warm with the temperature reaching 29 Celsius. We drove through lovely hilly country to see Rozhen Monastery situated up a steep hill. George ignored the 'Road closed' sign and drove up to near the entrance avoiding the collapsed section of road. This is a marvellous place, so peaceful and quiet. The original monastery was founded in the 12th or 13th century, but the present building dates from the sixteenth century as do the many wall paintings. Unfortunately no photography was allowed inside the church nor were there any postcards on sale so I was restricted to tasking photographs of the entrance gate and the main complex. There are now only three or four monks in residence. There were few visitors but one small group was being led by a lady who had been George's most unfavoured teacher when he had been doing his guide training, so we gave this group a miss.

Fresco above entrance gate of Rozhen Monastery. *Rozhen Monastery complex with church on right.*

We spent some time here before moving on to Melnik, the smallest town in Bulgaria. When Jacynth and I had visited it had been noted as the maker of the finest red wines in the country. The wines were still equally good but many other areas have now caught up in quality. Anyone who enjoys red wine should visit Bulgaria. While in Melnik we visited a large merchant's house, the largest in the Balkans, of the revivalist period, with its lavishly decorated rooms and Venetian stained glass windows, which has now been turned into a museum. It is clear from this building as well as other houses we visited in the country that many merchants flourished in Ottoman times despite the different religions, and the many churches remaining from those times show that the Christian religion was not only tolerated but often encouraged b the Muslim occupiers. Indeed some records show that some Muslim rulers paid for new churches to be built.

House Museum, Melnik.. *George standing in winery in museum house.*

The intention had now been to go and view an open air Roman site but looking out from our hill we could see that very heavy rain had developed over our destination, so we decided to return to Bansko, in the opposite direction, where the weather appeared more settled.

The next day we drove about twenty miles to the little village of Dobrasko which shelters a pearl of Bulgarian churches, St. Teodor Tyron and St. Teodor Stratilat. This church, set in a delightful garden, had been built in 1614 and its interior frescos, which cover the whole of the interior, painted at the same time. The fresco I liked most shows Christ ascending into heaven in what looks like a space rocket.

St. Teodor Tyron & St. Teodor Stratilat.   *Christ ascending into heaven.*

On our return to Bansko I was amused to see a sign to Hotel Elinor, the name of my daughter with the same spelling. We lunched in the open air at our hotel before going on to visit another museum house. Some of the wall paintings here were of Constantinople, as it was then called, showing ships equipped with both sails and steam.

Museum House, Bansko.

After this, since I had now free time, I walked down towards the bottom of the town to see the huge beautifully kept graveyard with its entrance covered with hundreds of Death Notices and photographs, Montenegrin style, many of them several years old. Next to the old railway station with the ancient engine and rolling stock still displayed on a siding as it had been so many years before.

I deserted the hotel for supper that night for I had found a delightful restaurant overlooking the statue to Father Paisil who had written the first History of Bulgaria. The food and wine were once again excellent and I also enjoyed the four piece band.

Bansko cemetery   *Old engine at Bansko station.*

The next day, a Saturday, there was a clear blue sky as we set off on our drive to Plovdiv but by the time we turned off the main road to go and see the museum mountain village of Kovatchevitsa it was raining and this continued as we drove up into the mountains through an alarming gypsy village. This was the one time during my whole holiday that I felt uncomfortable for it felt that if we had had to stop for any reason that we might well have been robbed. However we navigated the crowded street safely and by the time we reached our destination the rain had stopped though it was still damp when we descended from the car. This village was deserted but some of the houses are now being restored, several of them are occupied and a few of them apparently now offer bed and breakfast. On the way back down we stopped at another village, Leshten, which is slightly larger and boasts a church and a café with wonderful views where we stopped for a cup of coffee. Driving on down to the main road we discovered a new road had been built, bypassing the crowded and dirty gypsy village

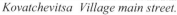

Kovatchevitsa Village main street.   *Leshten Village.*

We then regained the main road, stopping at the spa resort of Devin for lunch. There was not much sign of people taking the mineral waters and I, for one, contented myself with a Bulgarian beer.

Plovdiv is Bulgaria's second city the old town is built on one of several hills rising from the plain. My little hotel was situated up a narrow cobbled street. George left me there while he went off to visit his sister who lived in a newer part of the town and who had recently had a baby which he was anxious to see. I took advantage of some welcome sunshine to explore the cobbled streets around with the attractive painted houses as well as visiting a nearby church.

Plovdiv Old Town.

I finished the day by eating a meal in the hotel open air restaurant and saw the arrival of a German party which was shortly to be driven indoors by a heavy downpour. Luckily I had already finished my meal before the rain arrived.

Sunday seems to be a normal working day in Plovdiv and the morning was spent on foot. George's wife was also at breakfast since she had decided to spend the night here with George so she too could see the new baby. She then left for Kazanlak where their home was. The clouds soon cleared after the overnight rain and it became hot and sunny with the temperature reaching 32 Celsius.

We spent over three hours walking round Plovdiv, visiting churches, including one with small children charging around shouting during the service with no one trying to control them , and the Cathedral where a baptism and a wedding were taking place at the same time in different parts of the building and where the young children were being kept under a firm but friendly control. We also visited the lovely ethnographical museum in a fine 19th century house.

Ethnological Museum,Plovdiv.   *Plovdiv wedding.*

One of the things Plovdiv is most noted for is its Roman remains. Many of these, including the famous theatre, are situated on one side of the hill on which the Old Town stands, with views out over the main city. However some of them are situated in the main city itself and the Stadium runs along right underneath one of the principal streets. Only one end of it has been opened but near the other end there is a pedestrian underpass where a Roman

Villa, named Eirene, has been discovered and turned into a small underground museum filled with mosaics and other artefacts.

Roman Theatre, Plovdiv.

End of Roman Stadium, Plovdiv.

In Eirene Roman Villa Museum, Plovdiv.

We lunched in the Ernest Hemingway Restaurant before taking the car and driving out to see the Bachovo Monastery, the second largest monastery in Bulgaria. To get to the monastery we turned off the main road, which at that point was filled with parked cars and drove up a steep road lined with stalls on either side selling every kind of tourist tat. The road itself was also full of pedestrians. However George managed to drive up safely and find a parking space just outside the main entrance of the building. Through the main gate there were a number of visitors, though nothing like I had feared from the crowds outside. The Holy Mother of God Church, built in 1604, was full of fine frescos mainly painted in the 19th century. The light was not good so we had to stand long enough for our eyes to become accustomed to the gloom before we could really enjoy them at their best. It was the one building in the whole complex which was crowded, mainly with people queuing up to kiss the 14th century holy icon of St. Christopher. It would have taken us a long time to reach this holy relic so we did not linger there and went on to see some of the other buildings which were mercifully nearly empty. Indeed the refectory full of frescos including a wonderful Stem of Jesse stretching the whole length of the ceiling only had one other visitor during the whole time we were there.

Bachovo Monastery.   *Ceiling of refectory in Bachovo.*

On our return to Plovdiv I spent some time exploring the Roman remains and museums before, following the recommendation of George, taking supper in an open air restaurant near our hotel.

Monday started hot and sunny and remained so until the evening when it became cloudy, close and sticky. We set out for the Valley of the Roses where I was disappointed to find many of the rose fields past their best. Luckily when we reached the Rose Museum at Kazanlak there was still plenty of colour in their gardens. Over three thousand different species of rose are cultivated there. Rose oil is produced in large quantities in the season. George had met the president of L'Oreal who visits every year to make a new year's order for rose oil is used in all their products. The roses have to be picked from first light until about 10am when the sun gets too strong for them to retain their perfume. In Roman times many olive tree forests were destroyed to make room for rose bushes to be planted though it was not until the Middle Ages that it became possible to extract rose oil. It is a very difficult and arduous process even today and it is said that it takes 3,000 kilograms of red rose petals to make one litre of rose oil while 5,000 kilograms of white rose petals are needed for the same amount of oil. Not surprisingly today the price of one kilogram of rose oil is reckoned to cost 6,000 Euros.

Distilling rose oil   *Some of the roses in Kazanlak Rose Museum garden.*

This was followed by a visit to the Kazanlak Archaeological Museum which held mainly artefacts, both gold and bronze, including a gold face mask, found in some of the many Thracian tombs in the area.

Treasures from Thracian tombs in Kazanlak Archaeological Museum.

George, who lives in Kazanlak, took me to a Restaurant near the Kosyozarev Tomb, the most famous of the tombs, for lunch. Here the service as well as the food was excellent, possibly because George knew all the staff well. The taped music included, to my surprise and amusement, a Bulgarian version of 'Silent Night'. We then crossed a stream on foot and walked up to the Kosyozarev tomb. This was discovered in 1944 when the Bulgarian authorities were trying to mount anti-aircraft guns as protection of Karlovo and its gas tanking station from American bombing. The main surprise found in the tomb was the wall paintings which covered some of the walls and the inside of the domed roof. It was soon realised that unlimited access to this small building would cause damage to these paintings. Access is now allowed only to important visitors or, if there are none booked in, to a maximum of 17 on any day, first come first served. However an exact replica has been built only a short distance away for the benefit of visitors and George who has visited the original told me that the replica, which I went into, was very accurate. Luckily there was only one other visitor at the same time as me, for it was very small inside and it was impossible to walk around without brushing against the wall paintings. Although I knew it was not the real thing it gave a very good impression. The Thracian tombs in general date from the end of the fourth to the early years of the third centuries BC.

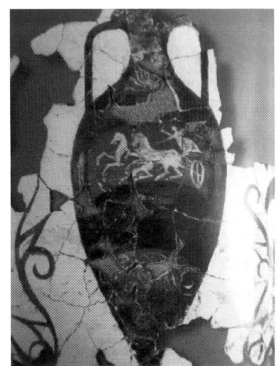

Kosyozarev Tomb Replica

We then drove back into Kazanlak where George parked the car in his own personal parking space before taking me to see another church and then to my hotel, the Palace, which proved to be a four star establishment instead of the three star I had been expecting. Apparently it had been three star until this year when the authorities decided that since for several years in succession it had won the annual competition in the country for the top three star hotel it should be moved up a grade. George told me that this was to the annoyance of the owners since it has not got the facilities to reach the top of its new grade. I had time before supper for a walk round Kazanlak, including a visit to the attractive park and another, but comparatively dull Church.

The next morning started with a surprise appearance of the Japanese lady who had been travelling round the country in a different direction and had found herself staying at this same hotel.

We started the day by driving some miles for an unscheduled visit to the tomb of Seuthus III whose bronze head I had seen, together with several other treasures found there, in the museum the previous day. This tomb, the real one and not a replica, was a little larger than the Kosyozarev and though it lacked the wall paintings I found it more impressive. There were no other visitors while I was there.

While we were driving to the tomb I had noticed the golden domes of some building glinting among the woodland on the edge of a mountain range which proved to be the Shipka Memorial Monastery of the Nativity of Christ and was to be the subject of our next visit. This truly Russian style building had been built in memory of the final defeat of the Ottomans at the Shipka Pass high up in the mountains above. Inside it contains the names of all those killed, Bulgarians, Russians, Ukrainians and others, but not of course the Ottomans, in the battle which led to the Treaty of St. Stefano establishing Bulgaria as a truly free independent country. I was frequently told of the important part played by the Russians in this fight for freedom and there did not appear to be any anti Russian feeling among the people I met.

The church itself stands well above the plain among woodlands. Even without its golden domes it would still be a remarkably elaborate building and it and its gardens are kept in a beautiful condition. I believe quite a lot of Russian money is used to help support it.

Shipka Monastery Memorial Church of the Nativity of Christ.

From this church we drove on up the steep mountain road for a considerable distance to the Shipka Pass where we parked some way below the actual memorial from where there are magnificent views in every direction.

Shipka Memorial on the Pass.

We then continued down the other side of the mountain until we reached an Anthropological museum to where a number of original village houses have been moved and rebuilt and in them are craftsmen and craftswomen all still practising their original trades using water power to work the simple machinery that they use. Many of their products are on sale at very reasonable prices and I bought an icon of St. Nicholas of Myra (Father

Christmas) which was painted by an old man using the traditional methods of icon painting. It was interesting to see him mixing his own paints from natural minerals and plants. There was no question of him buying pre made paints in tubes. Other crafts such as woodwork and ceramics depended entirely on the force of the water fed into their houses from the fast flowing stream down the steep hillside and then along through the middle of the village. There is also a pleasant café attached to the village where we stopped for lunch before driving on to the beautiful and peaceful 19th century nunnery and church at Sokolsky.

Anthropological Museum with icon painting.   *Sokolsky church.*

Finally we drove to Tryavna, an attractive little town noted for its woodcarving skills. We stopped at the little wood carving museum in a cobbled street. We had then intended to walk around the town but since it started raining we retreated to the car and drove to our hotel, the Ralitsa situated up a hill a little way out of the main town. Here I was given a fine suite with a large amount of carved wooden furniture and fittings. The only trouble with it was that the bed with its magnificent carved headboard was so low slung that it was almost impossible to stand up from. After a rest I decided, since the rain had now stopped, to walk down to the town and explore the cobbled streets which ran off from the main square, one of them over a fine humped back bridge, now pedestrian only, over the stream. Since rain once again threatened I then returned to the hotel.

Tryavna.

The hotel was hosting two schools that night and I had been warned that I might find the dining room rather noisy if I were to eat there but since the weather was so unsettled I decided to risk it. I was given a table on a small platform a little above the level of the main room. The noise was less than I had been prepared for, indeed I found it rather pleasant as a reminder of my many years teaching. However when the children had finished eating and left the room it was cleared and prepared for a disco. When they returned the noise increased considerably but since it was the first school disco I had attended for many years I found it most enjoyable, though I refused the efforts of a couple of children to get me to join in the dancing. I did feel sorry for one small boy who decided it was not his sort of thing and sat alone at another table on the platform playing some sort of game on his mobile phone.

It rained very heavily during the night and I was told that the previous night Sofia had suffered a normal half year's average rainfall in one night and that the weather system seemed to be coming our way. The rain had lessened to a drizzle when we left and by the time we reached Dryanovo Monastery, our next stop, it had almost ceased. The river running beside the monastery was rushing higher and faster than George had ever seen it and was only just below the level of the little footbridge we crossed. The position was lovely, with a steep cliff rising above it, but the church was very small and so dark it was difficult to distinguish the frescos inside. I was told it had declined in importance and that there were now only three or four nuns present. Quite a number of young visitors appeared, not to see the church but to visit the small adventure playground established in its garden.

Dryanovo Monastery.

We next travelled on to Veliko Turnovo. Here we were to encounter immediate problems. We went first to our hotel to book in but found that it was one of a number of places in the city which were without any water as a result of water main problems and would not accept us. George immediately rang up his firm who set about finding somewhere else for us, which he gathered might be a difficult task since several other hotels were in the same state. In the meantime we set off to look at some of the sights. During the course of our visiting he received a call back to say we were now booked in another hotel only just across the park from our original booking. When we arrived there we discovered it was only a two star establishment but it was clean, friendly and quite acceptable.

We first saw the outside of the Arts Museum and the impressive Monument to the Uprising against the Ottomans, before carrying on to the fortress of Tsarevets situated on a steep hill with its outer walls almost entirely surrounded by the Yantra river and the Church of the Patriarchate situated high on the top of the hill above the ruins of the Royal Palace. Here we parked the car outside the gateway, crossed the river by the causeway and climbed the hill through the ruins of the Royal Palace, which must once have been impressive buildings reminding one that in 1186 it had been the capital of the Second Bulgarian kingdom. The Patriarchate at the top has been fully restored and inside the walls are covered by striking new frescos whose artist is still living.

When we had returned through the outer gate George congratulated me and said that when he took a group there it was seldom that more than a quarter of the group went through the entrance gate let alone climbed up the hill to the top. There was a good restaurant nearby where we lunched before finding our new hotel which we reached just before another heavy shower.

Luckily the rain did not last long and after a rest I was able to take a walk. Veliko Turnovo is built on both side of a steep river valley, allowing for good views from most areas and is one of the more attractive cities I know. The majority of the houses are of the pleasant 19th century Bulgarian style. I walked across the park and soon found an attractive pedestrian precinct with many small shops.

Tsarevets Fortress .

Fresco in Patriachatw Church.

I also found a good restaurant near the hotel where we had originally been booked and only about five minutes walk across the park from our new lodging.

There was more heavy rain and thunder during the night but luckily the weather cleared while we were eating breakfast and George drove us out the see the village of Arbanassi. There is, I was told, a Bulgarian saying that if you have not visited the monasteries of Rila and Bachovo, seen Arbanassi and drunk Bulgarian plum brandy you have not experienced a full life. Personally I would substitute Bulgarian red wine for the plum brandy but otherwise there is a lot in this saying. Arbanassi is a lovely village in itself but the Church of the Nativity of Christ I count as one of the loveliest buildings I have ever seen. From outside it is nothing special but inside the frescos which cover the walls and the ceiling took my breath away.

Veliko Turnovo.   *Pedestrian precinct Veliko Turnovo*

The over 3,500 figures in this low barnlike church date from the 15th and 16th centuries and while it is by a long way the finest of the churches in Arbanassi several other churches there also have good frescos in them and are worth visiting. Indeed one could spend a full day visiting the village, its churches and several house museums, some of which we visited, whose size and evident wealth show how prosperous the place must have become in Ottoman times. It seems probable that the village benefited from taxes being removed in return for guarding the local mountain passes It was while we were walking through the churchyard that we met a small group who were being led by a man who proved to be the leader of George's body of guides and who stopped to speak to George and to ask me If I was being well treated. He seemed pleased when I said, truthfully, that I could not have a better guide. His group, George told me, was a body of important Bulgarian officials.

Frescos from the Church of the Nativity, Arbanasi.

The village is one of the few local mountain villages which appears to have survived unscathed from the frequent earthquakes. I noticed that many of the buildings were built with occasional horizontal layers of wooden beams between the stones, which I have seen elsewhere in earthquake prone areas, as a protection.

Our next visit was to be to the Preobrazhenie Monastery Transfiguration of Our Lord. This was not on our itinerary but George thought it was a visit I would like and as usual he proved to be right. To reach it we had to drive back through Veliko Turnovo and then for several miles along a narrow wooded valley. This had originally been a training monastery for new priests but unfortunately it had been built on unstable ground and there had also been a bad rock fall from the cliff above which had rendered all the living quarters unsafe. The church itself was very lucky to have been saved since two large boulders are still lying where they had fallen, one on each side of the church, only inches away from the walls. As a result though it retains the name of a monastery no one now lives there and it is just used as a church.

Preobrazhenie Monastery Transfiguration of Our Lord and external fresco.

While we were there another visitor appeared who proved to be the Archbishop of Veliko Turnovo, the second highest ranking priest in Bulgaria. He spoke excellent English and told me he had come to visit here since it was where he had done his early training to be a priest. ,He also told me he had been a member of a committee set up to try to improve relations between the Anglican and Orthodox communities and had met my then Bishop of Bath and Wells.

On our return to Veliko Turnovo George and I lunched in a city centre restaurant before I set out by myself on a long walk during the course of which I took a closer look at the striking Monument to the Uprising and spent some time in the Arts Museum as well as exploring some of the old attractive streets.

Monument to the Uprising.

Veliko Turnovo Streets scene.

Much of my walk was in sunshine but when the clouds built up I hastily made my way back to my hotel which I reached shortly before one of the most violent thunder storms I have ever known broke. Luckily it only lasted about an hour so when the rain stopped I decided to go to the same restaurant that I had visited the previous night. When I reached the lobby the man at the reception desk advised me not to leave yet. I asked why since the rain had stopped and he just pointed outside. When I looked out I saw that the street there had become a fast flowing river and I had to wait another hour or so before I was able to start out. I had another excellent meal and also met an English woman who had brought her mother with her as a seventy first birthday treat, two of the few British tourists I met during my whole holiday.

There was some more heavy rain during the night, but luckily it had stopped before we set off to the Troyan Monastery, the third largest in Bulgaria. Once again there were marvellous frescos which were being restored from the layers of black soot caused by hundreds of years of candle smoke. Many of them had by now been cleaned and we were able to watch the restorers at work. Those not yet cleaned were almost invisible and I was pleased I had not made the trip a year earlier.

Frescos in the Troyan Monastery.

We then drove over a high pass, through lovely Alpine type scenery, as well as some hill fog, to the mountain village of Koprivshtitsa where we first stopped for lunch at a café in the centre. Since some more heavy rain started at this point we then drove directly to our hotel on a hillside on the outskirts of the village. The hotel lived up to its name, the Panorama, for when the rain ceased there were lovely views over the surrounding countryside. When the rain had eased off we set out on foot to explore the village where as we reached the centre again the clouds suddenly cleared and we had warm sunshine.

This proved to be a lovely village with its 19th century architecture painted in many different colours. Several of the houses have been turned into museums and we visited some of these, including the little blue house which, built by his grandfather, was the birthplace home of the poet Duncho Debelyanov which holds copies of many of his books. There is also a moving little statue in the garden showing his mother sitting there waiting for him to return from the war. He never did return for he was killed in Greece in 1916. There are many memorials of the uprising against the Ottomans in 1876 which led to the freedom of Bulgaria, for it was here that the first Turk was killed, on the little humpbacked bridge across the stream and the leader of the April Rising, Todor Kableshkov, lived in a house nearby. We spent over two and a half hours on our walk, and could well have spent more. One sight, which I did not get a chance to photograph, was a long string of horses, tethered together being led in line by one man, for the horse is still an important part of life here.

Statue of Duncho's mother.

For our last full day we drove back to Sofia, through lovely countryside, and parked outside the Aleksandur Nevski Memorial Church outside which there was a large exhibition of old cars and motor bicycles. We then went to the crypt of the church, where I had not been on our earlier visit, which had been turned into a large, possibly the world's largest, Icon Museum. The exhibits varied from very early icons up until the 19th century.

I was then deposited back at the hotel and after a short rest took another walk to the centre visiting the National Art Museum when rain threatened. There were some lovely rooms though the exhibits were not of a high standard except for an exhibition of children's art which suggests that there is hope for the artistic future of Bulgaria.

I ended up my tour by an excellent meal at the same restaurant as before .Despite the unsettled weather it had been another marvellous holiday of visits, food, wine and my wonderful guide.

Chapter Three

Kurdistan: A country in the Making

The Iraqi flag with the Kurdistan crown imposed.

When I told anyone that I was going to Iraqi Kurdistan the immediate question was not about what I hoped to do or to see but "Is it safe?" I felt reasonably happy about this since it was the one part of Iraq which the Foreign Office seemed to have no reservations about, though when a car bomb went off in the capital, Erbil, five days before we were due to travel I was afraid the tour company might be required to call the trip off. Luckily this, the first act of terrorism for six years, proved to be a one off and at the time of writing there has been nothing further.

The group, some eighteen strong plus our manager, Peter, met at Heathrow and I found that I knew about half of them from previous trips with the same company, Eastern Approaches. The flight, very early in the morning, was on time but none of us enjoyed the change of planes at Vienna where we had to go through three security checks and to walk very long distances with no moving tracks. The meal, however, was excellent for an airline meal.

When we arrived our luggage was piled into one mini bus and us into another. We had to stop for a time when one of the party thought he had lost his passport at the airport, but luckily he found it in a different pocket. None of us had any idea of what the hotels would be like but this one which had an official 4* rating was what I would describe as good 3* by European standards, so I had no complaints. The check in was very slow but we were eventually all settled in our rooms. After a short rest we were collected by our Kurdistani guide, Shakri, and taken out to an excellent open air restaurant for a Lebanese Mezze style supper though without any alcohol. The music included a version of "Happy birthday to you," though it was not meant for any of us. I was surprised to find that back in our hotel we had English style square three pin electric plug holes.

The next day was to start in an unexpected fashion. We were driven to the Ministry of Tourism, which was not on our scheduled itinerary. Shakri explained that the Minister of Tourism himself wanted to meet us. The drive there through the city showed a tremendous amount of rebuilding taking place with building after building covered in scaffolding. When we arrived our coach was not allowed through the gates, which were guarded by armed soldiers so we had to park outside. When we walked through the entrance we were met by a range of television cameras before we were ushered into a large board room with a long table where we sat while TV and press reporters sat on chairs around the edges of the room. We were all given a bottle of water, and later on a glass of tea. There were also small gifts for each of us including a tourist map and a large desk diary, which would have been very useful if it had been for the next year. Eventually the Minister appeared, took the chair at the head of the table and welcomed us. He told us a little about Kurdistan and explained that it was a semi autonomous province with its own Parliament of one hundred and eleven members and had its own army and police force We were then asked if we had any questions the first one of which, not by me, explained how many of us had been asked if it was safe. We were told very firmly that it was absolutely safe.

After a few more questions the Minister had to leave and his deputy took over answering more questions in the course of which we were given the impression that, though there had been a few visitors before and a small archaeological group we were the first proper foreign tourist group ever to have visited since the Iraq Iran war.

When we were released outside we were approached by the Press and TV and several of us, especially our manager, Peter were interviewed about why we had come to visit and what we hoped to see while we were in the country. We all gained the impression that all the Kurds hoped to gain complete independence within the next few years.

Meeting at the Tourism Ministry, Erbil.   *Peter being interviewed for Kurdistan TV.*

The weather was now cloudless and indeed we had perfect weather for the whole of our trip since for the first five days there was literally not a cloud in the sky and even after that only a very few high white clouds which never obscured the sun despite which the temperature was never too great for comfort. We were first driven to the small Museum of Civilisation, guarded as were all the museums, by armed soldiers. We were allowed to photograph only in the lobby where several archaeologists were at work piecing some artefacts together. The exhibits themselves were interesting and gave us some idea of what we were to see later in our trip.

Museum of Civilisation, Erbil.

Guard to Museum.

We were next driven to the Citadel which towers over the city. Here we had to wait for sometime, in the coach, while Shakri phoned, on his mobile, to get permission for the coach to drive us up the steep hill and into the entrance. Permission was eventually granted and the coach, when it reached the top had to do considerable manoeuvring to make the sharp turn through the gate with only inches to spare. We were told afterwards that we were the largest coach ever to have been allowed to make that journey. Inside the wall all the houses are being restored and all the inhabitants have had to be moved until the work has been done. We heard that when the work was completed some but not all of them would return to their old homes. While there we visited the old baths, a mosque and several of the restored houses one of which has been turned into a shop selling typical Kurdistan goods including scarves, jewellery and ceramics. There were even a few books about Kurdistan, the only ones I was to see during the trip. Since these books were expensive and their photographs not of good quality I did not buy any.

Mosque and Bath house in Citadel.

Restored House in Citadel

Base of Minaret.   *View from Minaret Garden.*

After lunch we had been scheduled to visit the new Syriac Museum but were told that this was not open because of the exhibits being entirely reorganised, so instead we were taken to see the famous hexagonal minaret set in a fine large garden with statuary. Our driver had some difficulty in finding this but eventually he found the entrance to the garden, which was at the opposite end to the minaret. However the walk through the garden made the whole visit very worthwhile.

The day finished with an excellent meal, with wine included, and a sort of music I had never heard before even in the East.

The next day we were meant to start off at 8.00 am but we were delayed for a long time by the late arrival of the eighteen and nineteen year old two children of the Manager of Marjan our local travel company who were to travel with us on that day. We were first taken to see the badly defaced rock carving high up on a mountain cliff above the village where we had to park our coach. There was no path up to the carving so the majority of us, including the two youngsters, decided it was not worth while making the climb and waited down below. We were soon found by several young children who gathered round us, most of them never having seen foreigners before, who were pleased to practise the small amount of English they had learnt at school.

During our whole trip tp Kurdistan we frequently found ourselves greeted with "What is your name?" usually followed up with "How old are you?" Very seldom did the conversation get any further since our replies were usually greeted by a stunned silence.

Our next trip,was to see the Shanidar Cave which was easier to reach, though even this involved a long uphill trek including over three hundred steps, but the surface was good. This is a limestone cave some 750m above sea level and is very important because of the

remains are now all in museums, but the site itself is remarkable and the view from it out over the plateau very fine.

Route up to Shanidar Cave.   *Shanidar Cave,*

After our descent we had a long drive to the fish restaurant owned by Shakri's brother. Here we had a two hour wait for our meal, and we had already arrived late. The meal of fresh fish when we were eventually served was excellent but since we had to drive back past the cave and then the cliff carving in order to reach our final visit of the day, the Rawanduz Gorge, we all of us felt somewhere else could have been found to eat, especially since there were several cafes in a village near the gorge and by the time we reached the gorge evening was fast drawing in and dusk falling. After our first stop near a waterfall in the gorge we were driven on to see the original road bridge which was now in almost complete darkness before being driven back up the gorge and onto the road back to Erbil. Peter, with our support vetoed a suggestion that we should go out to another restaurant in Erbil and we ate a very satisfactory meal in the hotel. The whole experience was a learning one for Shakri who was used to driving oil magnates around in saloons but had not before taken a foreign group. Luckily he was a fast learner, a very nice person and by the end a good guide.

Evening drive towards Rawanduz gorge.   *Waterfall at gorge.*

We had to leave at 8.am again the next morning to drive to drive to Suleimani, Kurdistan's second city with stops on the way. We had already found that a considerable amount of extra time had to be allowed on any journey for the continual army and police road blocks, at many of which we all had to show our passports. There were to be even more of these on this journey for near Kirkuk we had for a short time to leave Kurdistani territory into Iraq proper before crossing into another part of Kurdistan again. At both crossing points we had to pass through two road blocks run by Kurdistani and Iraqi soldiers respectively. The area round Kirkuk is one of the main oil production areas of Iraq and we saw many oil wells and a large majority of traffic on the roads was made up of oil tankers. We were told that the number of these would soon be reducing as an oil pipe was being built to the Turkish coast in the Eastern Mediterranean.

Our first stop, after the border crossing, was to see the remains of a fortified Nestorian church, built in Sasanian times, dating from the fifth century, at Bazyan as well as a fortress in the same place.

Bazyan fortress.   *Ruins of Nestorian Church at Bazyan.*

Our next stop was at Halabja at the monument to the victims of the gas attack by Saddam Hussein in his fight with the Kurds. The monument itself was closed for complete restoration and was enclosed in scaffolding. We had to park some way away and were not originally allowed through the entrance gate. However after some telephoning we were first allowed to walk through the gates and up to view the monument at close quarters. The sixteen fingers on the monument refer to the date of the month and the hands point to the month of the year. The bubbles below these are meant to represent the blisters which appeared on the skin of those affected by the gas. The authorities were then, after a time, persuaded to allow us into the little museum which mainly consisted of photographs taken during and after the attack. Many of these were horrifying showing the corpses of victims as well as some, including children, suffering under treatment for their terrifying injuries. Also it contained the death warrant of 'Chemical Ali' who was responsible for the attack together with the pen with which the warrant was signed. In addition to this there was displayed the actual rope with which he was hanged beside a photograph of the man himself. Altogether it proved to be a very interesting and sobering visit, even if it certainly could not be described as an enjoyable one, as indeed how could so many people endure their fellow

After a late lunch we carried on to our hotel in Suleimani, stopping to view a large Tel on the way. Shagri wanted us to climb up to the top but Peter said "No" very firmly since it was already getting dark. Our 5* hotel proved to be very close to a European 5* and would have reached that standard had it not been for the poor checking in procedure and the fact that the switch for the bed light could not be reached from the bed. The food was excellent and since it was the eighty fifth birthday of one of our group (there were at least two members of the group older than me!) a special birthday cake was produced.

The following day started with a visit to the Archaeological Museum of Suleimani, the second largest museum in the whole of Iraq. This was officially closed for reorganisation but Shakri managed to have it opened just for us. This was an excellent visit made even more enjoyable since we were the only visitors there and thus were able to take our leisure and were allowed to photograph the exhibits, of which there was a great variety, including some ancient cuneiform writing carved into rock.

Some of the exhibits in the Archaeological Museum of Sulemani.

Our next visit was of a very different nature. The prison, in which Sadam Hussein had incarcerated Kurdish prisoners had been turned into a museum. The entrance corridor had walls and ceiling made of small shards of glass, over five thousand of them, one for each Kurd killed in the infamous gas attack. Apart from one area which had incongruously been turned into a carpet museum, the rooms, some of them so tiny it would have been impossible to lie down in, had been kept as cells in which men, women and children had been held and in some of them Madam Tusaud type models have been placed. The most horrible of these show prisoners being tortured.

Sadam Hussein's Prison for Kurds.

Outside the actual building there was an ancient tank and some other old military vehicles which had been captured by the Kurds in the fighting. Several small children were climbing over these. I only hope they were not allowed inside the building itself.

We next stopped near a supermarket in order to buy a picnic lunch. A few went to do the shopping while the rest of us soon found ourselves guarding the coach for the driver had disappeared leaving it unlocked. After this work was satisfactorily completed our driver reappeared and we drove into the mountains to visit the Achaemenid cave tomb of Qizqapan. The bus had to park well below the tomb and we had to climb up a steep path to reach the site itself. The final bit was up a number of steps up a tall freestanding metal structure to a platform with a gap some six feet wide with a sheer drop of some fifty feet below covered by a rickety piece of hardboard if one wished to enter the tomb itself. Only one member of the group, pictured, was brave or rash enough to actually cross this rickety bridge.

Quizqapan cave tomb. *Ian returning from the tomb.*

By now we were all feeling very hungry and it was getting quite late in the afternoon so we decided to eat our picnic lunch in a wood by a stream in the valley below which proved a delightful spot.

View from Qizqapan down to coach in middle distance. *Picnic spot.*

We ate in the hotel that evening and several of us decided to share a bottle of wine having first being quoted a price of 7,000 dinars by the waiter. When the bill for the wine arrived we found it was being charged at 18,000 dinars. I argued about this and was told that as they had found they were out of the wine we had ordered they had given us this one instead and this was its cost. Eventually the manager was called and after an argument we only had to pay the original quoted cost and some others who had already paid were refunded some of their money. Whether it was a real mistake or an attempted scam on their part I do not know.

The next day we set off for the city of Dohuk where we first went to visit the citadel and caravanserai of Koya Qishla. This was firmly locked shut, apparently for the Muslim festival of Eid, but after some telephoning the guard was allowed to open it for us. During the 19th century this had been the Ottoman headquarters of the region and through the gates was a huge square with buildings attached to the outer walls, one side of which had been turned into a museum, and in one corner stood a little mosque with a green tiled dome. After a time the curator arrived and we were taken into his office for a talk on the building. After this he opened up the museum for us, and said he himself would shortly have to leave on business However he obviously decided we were more important for after quite a time at the museum he led us into the town to see a large house which was being restored as the cultural centre of Koya, for which he was also responsible. He then led us to the bazaar which also proved interesting, for though many of the shops were closed for religious reasons quite a lot of it which was in ruins was being restored.

Here we met a small group of Czechoslovakian architects we had already met in the Erbil museum. Talking to them we found that they had come to Kurdistan to help restore houses. After a stop for a refreshing cup of tea in the bazaar we said goodbye to our curator and set off for Shaqlawa to visit a rock cut Assyrian Christian cave monastery. The road up to this place was too steep and narrow for our coach so at the town we had to transfer to minibuses which took us much of the way.

When we reached the parking area we used its wall for a picnic lunch, very late in the afternoon, after walking up to the almost defunct ruin, from where the view, though fine, was very little different from what we could see from our luncheon wall.

Koya Citadel

66

Meeting with Koya Curator.

Koya Citadel Museum.

New Cultural Centre House, Koya

Koya Bazaar being restored.

Our drive to Dohuk was now scheduled to take 2 hours but in fact it took nearly twice as long. Our coach only just managed to get through the entrance gates when we arrived after dark since several cars were parked badly. The hotel was officially 5* but to my mind it only reached the middle standard of a 2* establishment. However a good beer at dinner was very fine value price wise.

There were actually a few white clouds in the sky when we set out, the next day, for a mainly Christian village, called Alqosh, to see the Assyrian monastery of Mar Rabban Hormizd or Notre Dame des Semences (Our Lady of the Seeds) as it is now called. Here most of the buildings were fairly new since the monastery had moved, in 1859, with financial help by the Vatican, from its original position up in the cliffs several kilometres away. We had to pass through several road blocks on the way since once again we had to travel into Iraq proper where Alqosh, protected by Iraqi, not Kurdistani troops, lies, with Mosul, a scene of occasional terrorism, less than thirty miles away

The main courtyard courtyard, full of flowers and birds, was an oasis of calm. We were shown round by a priest who told us of attacks during the recent troubles when many of the buildings had been damaged and a monk killed. Now most of the buildings had been rebuilt and housed some eighty monks as well as an orphanage holding eighteen orphans. The monastery also did a lot of work helping and feeding the poor. Much of the money for this was given by the Muslim Kurdish government. I think that the Kurds who have themselves suffered so much persecution in the past have developed a great feeling for their own minorities whatever their beliefs.

We were then loaded into minibuses for the journey up the steep and very windy narrow road to a small flat area below the cliff upon, and in, which the original monastery was built in the 7th century by Rabban Hormizd. Before the end of the 15th century it had become the patriarchal burial site and then until the 18th century the residence of the patriarchs of the oldest and largest patriarchal See of the Church of the East. We now had to climb over a hundred steps to reach the monastery. Here we found that much restoration was being done, and the little church had been completely rebuilt, though many of the cave cells on different levels involving a lot more climbing, remained in a ruined state. While we were there a local girls' choir arrived on a visit and we enjoyed some beautiful singing. One of the cells had been converted into a little café and we sat and enjoyed glasses of tea before leaving.

New Monastery   *Café in cave cell in old monastery.*   *Old monastery of Hormizd.*

We drove back through Dohuk, where we stopped for lunch at a café with the quickest service I have ever met, before driving on to Zakho near the Turkish border where we visited an early Ottoman arched stone bridge over a tributary of the Tigris river.

Early Ottoman bridge at Zakho.

After watching the sunset over the bridge from a nearby café we drove back to our hotel at Dohuk. I found that my room had not been cleaned during the day. I reported this to the desk and when I returned after dinner I found that they had listened to me and a cleaner had been sent in. A few of the party had taken a taxi into town to see the bazaar and eat there but I gathered that the majority of us had done better by staying in the hotel.

The next day was to be the first day of the Muslim holiday of Eid and we wondered if this would affect us. We drove to the medieval walled town of Amedi set on a mountain top with marvellous views. At the entrance to the town there was a notice forbidding the taking of sheep inside, however near where we parked our coach tied to a lampost was an unhappy looking animal which was destined to be slaughtered soon for the feast due that evening. Though most of the shops were closed we were able to walk to see the original town gate with its carvings on a steep and very rough path. Above the path there was a very worn carved relief on the cliff face.

Almedi town gate.

Carved relief near Almedi town gate.

Later we walked further round the town when we were all invited into a family home for tea, water and biscuits. A number of other inhabitants appeared while we were there for it is the custom in Amedi to invite friends and neighbours in during Eid. On the wall were photos of several family members who had fought in the war against Sadam, and three of them had been hanged when they had been captured by Sadam's forces. One of these men was an officer in the Kurdish army who had been trained at Sandhurst. We were later to see a bust of him erected in a place of honour in the town.

On our way back to Dohuk we stopped for lunch at an open air café where the excellence of the food was a very strong contrast to the squalid state of the WCs. This was the only time where we did not find places which were reasonably clean. We did not stop at the hotel in Dohuk but drove on the bypass and then on a road up into the mountains overlooking the city.

Airconditioning in house ii Amedi.   *Soldier Memorial.*

Our aim was to find some fine Assyrian rock reliefs at Maltai. We were stopped by soldiers at a road block and were told that they had strict instructions not to let any foreigners or unauthorised people to go any further. After telephoning back to Dohuk we were told to wait and after half an hour a taxi arrived carrying an official after which we were allowed to scramble down the steep hillside for several hundred feet and then round a corner with no track after a very short distance. The carved reliefs, when eventually discovered were very fine, one of them showing Sennacherib in the assembly of the gods. Considerably better access needs to be made before they become the attraction they deserve.

The route to Maltai reliefs.   *One of the Maltai reliefs.*

Our final full day was to be a very long one for we were to make several very interesting visits on our way back to Erbil. The first was to the centre of the Yesidi religion at Lalish. The Yesidi religion is unusual. It is followed by some 200,000 Kurds, over half of them living in Iraq. Dating from about the start of the 12th century from a Muslim Sufi brotherhood it developed into a fully fledged religion containing elements of Muslim, Jewish, Christian and Zoroastrian beliefs. Among its tenets is a belief that Satan, the fallen angel, actually repented of his evil ways, was forgiven by god and became a saint. Any member of this church is only allowed to marry another member with the result that they all look rather alike and it is said can always recognise another co-religionist by their physical appearance whenever they meet them anywhere in the world.. The Muslim holiday of Eid is also a holiday for them as result of which when we visited the number of pilgrims visiting, of all ages, must have been over a thousand. Families were camping in different rooms and were cooking their own food on little fires built on the concrete floor. Because there were so many there we had to park well down the hill before walking up to the entrance where we took off our shoes and socks while waiting for a guide. We proved to be something of a sensation and quite a number stood and watched while Shakri translated the guide's talk to us. We were then led further up the complex and the number of onlookers increased, many of them climbing onto roofs to listen in. We gathered that until recently all instruction was passed on orally and written tradition is very new.

Yezidi Shrines in Lalish.

Interested Yezidi Onlookers

Ezidi ady waiting to Baptise Infants

Yezidi Man at Temple Entrance.

Yezidi Child.

Yezidi Pilgrim Family.

It was interesting to see that there were armed Kurdish soldiers guarding the complex and to hear that the Kurdish government also pays money to help this unusual group. We spent some time, individually, walking round the complex and talking with those who could speak English before leaving to go and see Bavian where there is an Assyrian rock relief showing King Sennacherib at the start of the remarkable aqueduct built by him to carry water to Ninevah. The river itself was a most beautiful blue colour. There were also some other carvings visible on rocks near the river and parts of the canal can be seen with water still in it.

Jirwana proved more difficult to reach. We were supposed to have minibuses arrive to take us to the site up a track from the road. When these did not arrive our coach driver said he thought he could manage the track. However halfway along some construction work was taking place and drainage pipes were lying across the road so we had to dismount and make the rest of our way on foot. This was the place where the remains of the aqueduct itself crossed a valley and is particularly interesting for the cuneiform inscriptions carved into the stonework recording in Senacherib's own words how he would be remembered forever for this particular construction.

Bavian. Carving of King Senacherib.

Bavian. Animal carving.

Track to Jirwana.   *Ruins of Jirwana aqueduct.*

It is believed that Alexander's great victory over the Persians took place at Jirwana but no remains of the battle have been found.

We stopped for our lunch at a wayside café, at about 4pm, before setting out for Erbil. This journey took longer than expected since we had to spend a full hour each time passing through two road blocks, one by the army and the other by the police, on the way into the city. By the time we returned we decided unanimously not to go out to a restaurant and ate in the hotel.

A road block on the way back to Erbil.

On our final morning we were driven into the centre, below the citadel, so that we might explore the bazaar individually. It was an attractive area though the most interesting thing I saw was a shop keeper apparently guarding his shop with a rifle slung over his shoulder.

When we returned to the hotel we found a television crew waiting for us to discover how we had found our holiday. Peter pulled me out to be interviewed with him saying I had sufficient gravitas! We then drove off to lunch in a restaurant near to the airport. Our flight home, with the usual change of planes at Vienna made for an uneventful end to the holiday.

Erbil. Shop keeper with rifle.   *Erbil minaret near bazaar.*

Erbil. Bazaar.

Chapter 4.

Algeria : A Tour under Police Guard.

Statue in Guelma Roman Theatre.

My first trip of 2014 was to be to Algeria. Before I was able to book for this trip the agents with whom I had not previously travelled demanded a note from my GP, because of my age, saying that I was fit to follow this itinerary. I had not seen my GP in person for some five years having only had to visit her surgery for anti flu and updating travel jabs. However she gave me some quick tests, read hastily through the itinerary and immediately sent off an e-mail saying she was quite happy for me to do this tour. Later I was sent a new itinerary, with various changes in it, to submit with my visa application. These preliminaries having been completed well before our leaving date I received yet another itinerary which I assumed would be the last.

The flight was early in the morning so that I had to leave my Gatwick hotel at 0500 am to catch the plane. Luckily the flight took only just over two hours arriving at 11.00 local time. There now proceeded to be a period of chaos at the passport control. The official at my desk demanded my itinerary, and having studied it carefully, took it and my passport away to be checked by higher authority. I soon realised that the same problems were happening at other desks. Eventually all the members of our group were led off together to wait until matters were sorted out. After a time we were allowed to collect our luggage but we then had to wait some time longer for our passports to be returned. Finally we were allowed out and were able to meet our guide, Erwin, who had been waiting patiently for us. There was now another long delay so that all fifteen of us could change currency at the money exchange office.

On the way to the hotel Safir Erwin informed us that the itinerary had yet again been changed and that instead of spending two nights in Algiers we would be leaving by the 7.00am flight to Annaba the next morning and that we would be spending more time in Algiers at the end of the trip. We were also told that various places we had been going to visit might now be off limits and we would not necessarily know from day to day where our next trip would take us since there were supposed to be considerable tensions in some areas due to presidential elections which were to take place shortly.

The hotel Safir proved to be in an excellent position overlooking the sea with large rooms which were now starting to show their age. We were given plenty of time to settle in and I was able to go out and find a suitable café for a light lunch. After this we were taken to see the Archaeological and the Museum of Islamic Art, both of which buildings were in the same garden up near the top of a hill overlooking the city. To our surprise we found that the whole area was overrun by school children and their teachers. We discovered that this was a special day marking the recent return from Tunisia of the statue of a Gorgon's head which had been stolen from Hippo Regius in 1996. The Minister of Education was attending as well as many schools. Luckily the proceedings were just coming to an end as we arrived and we soon had the area almost to ourselves. There was also a benefit to us since the normal ban on photography had been raised for the day, though not in the Museum of Islamic Art. Apart from the returned head there were many fine Roman mosaics and sculptures. Indeed the number of mosaics everywhere we visited was truly remarkable and possibly as fine as those to be found in Tunisia, though photography was not allowed in most of the museums and quality postcards of the exhibits were seldom to be found even if postcards were to be found at all.

After a good time here we were driven to the very top of the hill overlooking the whole city to see the huge modern Martyrs' Memorial statue. This was remarkably similar in style and shape to the Freedom Monument in Tehran, though considerably larger and more imposing.

Returned Gorgon's Head.

Mosaic in Archaeological Museum, Algiers.

Martyrs' Memorial, Algiers.

On the way down back to the hotel I noticed we were following a police car with flashing blue lights. I originally imagined that our driver had cleverly taken the chance of following this car and thus cutting through the heavy traffic and it was only

actually leading us, and when we reached the hotel and the police car drew up in front of us it was even more obviously the case. At supper we were told that our coach would always be accompanied by the local police and that there might be delays when we crossed provincial borders and the new car might not yet have arrived to take over. In fact the replacement car was almost always waiting for us and there was only one occasion on which there was a real delay.

At supper I discovered that Sally, one of our party, had been up at Somerville College, Oxford at the same time as Jenny, one of my younger sisters though she had not known her well.

We were up very early again for our flight to Annaba, though the hotel produced an early breakfast before we left. At the airport itself we had to fill in further lengthy registration forms before flying. However the forty five minute flight was on time and when we arrived we were met by the same coach and driver of the previous day who had evidently driven overnight. We drove first, accompanied again by a police car, to the old Roman site of Hippone which had been opened early for us. We first walked up a low hill to see the small museum with many artefacts which had been recovered by the French in the original excavation. We then walked down to the site itself which was being cleared and weeded again after many years of neglect. Photography of the site was not allowed, it was the only site we visited where this prohibition took place, though since we were allowed to take photographs of the Basilica of St, Augustine of Hippo which stood on the top of a steep hill above the site, it was impossible to avoid some pictures of the remains appearing in the foreground while showing the church in the background. As well as our police guards there were a large number of security men as well as the workers in evidence. We were shown the place from where the Gorgon's head had been stolen though no one knew whether it would be returned from Algiers. The whole was very atmospheric, especially the flooded forum which stood near to the hill on which the basilica stood.

Flooded Roman Forum of Hippone below Basilica of St. Augustine of Hippo.

We had plenty of time for exploring the forum and I had a long conversation with one of the workmen who told me they hoped to finish clearing the site by the end of the summer. We were next driven up to the Basilica of St. Augustine of Hippo itself. The church had been built in the late nineteenth century in memory of the famous saint and had recently undergone considerable restoration. From there we were driven to a coastal café where we were able to sit for some time basking in the sun and overlooking a sparkling sea while drinking a cup of coffee, or in my case a glass of excellent orange juice. It was while we were here that we learnt that Sue, the lively Australian member of our group would be leaving us to fly back to Australia where her step daughter had suddenly been taken very ill and was dying. It was unclear whether she would be able to get back in time to see her alive. A week later we had an e-mail to say she had arrived in time to spend a couple of days with her before she died. We also learnt that our itinerary for the next day was having to be changed under police orders since tensions might boil over in the place we had been due to visit.

This was because it was the home town of one of the presidential candidates.

We were then taken to our hotel and after we had settled into our rooms out to a nearby café where we had a good lunch, in my case a delicious brique, despite a long wait for orders to be delivered. We were later to visit the same café for our supper at the end of which the owner insisted on taking a photograph of our group. We believed this was for publicity purposes.

In the afternoon we took a walk through Annaba and its crowded streets. It proved to be an attractive town with many fine nineteenth century style houses.

Basilica of St. Augustine of Hippo.

Typical Annaba house.

We ended up in a wine bar but after a tasting I was not tempted to buy any of their products. It was next proposed to visit a market but after a quick look I decided it was not up to the standard of many I had seen so thought I would return to the hotel. I told Erwin what I was going to do so that he would not waste time looking for me in case I was lost. He told me that Feisal, the manager of the Algerian company that was looking after us and who had joined us for the whole of our trip was also returning and would show me the way. I said I was perfectly capable of finding my own way but Feisal insisted on going with me. This was the first time that I saw the efforts by those in authority to make sue that all the tourists in the country should be kept safe. We all came to find this care a bit oppressive.

The next day we were given a longer lie in and it was not until the reasonable hour of 9am that we left for Guelma, accompanied by a police car. When we crossed the provincial boundary we found a new police car ready waiting for us. Our first visit was to the large Roman theatre in Guelma which, with a considerable amount of Roman statuary, both in the museum and in the little garden outside, was very interesting despite considerable restoration, as was the Mosaic museum which was seldom opened and neither Erwin nor our Algerian guide had ever been inside it before. Though small it had several mosaics including an exceptional one of Venus with fishermen and countless fishes. Unfortunately no photography was allowed and there was nothing in the way of pictures or postcards. We were next taken to an archaeological garden where many Roman artefacts from the town had been placed. Once again there was to be no photography due to the fact that one of the exactly similar houses surrounding the garden was apparently a military establishment. Finally we went to see the Roman Great Baths, where photography was allowed. Here we were joined by a number of children who though much interested by the unusual sight of foreigners did not pester us in any way.

The Roman Theatre, Guelma.

Lunch was taken after we had been settled into our rooms in the pleasant hotel in Guelma before we set out on our afternoon trip to the Roman remains at Thibisti. This was not on our original list of places to visit and I would have been sorry to have missed it for it was a superb forty five hectare site set in a lovely deserted area which had been excavated by the French in the early 20th century and little touched since they had left and so was overgrown with wild flowers.

Roman site of Thibisti.

Thursday was to be a very full day. We started by driving to see the hot springs at Hammam Meskoutime. These are obviously a very popular local attraction and when we arrived there were already a large number of visitors, though we appeared to be the only foreigners there. Wewere told later that we were the only foreign tour group in the country at the time, though a French group was supposed to be arriving just after we had left. How the police would manage if a number of groups turned up at the same time I do not know.

Hot springs near Guelma.

At the bottom of the springs there were kept on display a couple of peacocks as well as a poor monkey which did not appear to have been washed for a considerable time since its fur had become completely discoloured by the coloured steam emanating from the spring. We then walked up to the top and entered past several stalls selling mementoes onto the flat top of the spring with steam rising all round us and streams of hot water running through. There was a considerable unpleasant sulphuric smell all around the place but it was certainly interesting. It is said that apart from the hot springs in Iceland it is the second hottest spring in the world with water rising from the ground at a temperature of just under 100 degrees Celsius. Some of the buildings around have Roman baths that are still in use today. We than had a brief stop at the Mausoleum of Manisi which reminded me of the base of the Tomb of Cyrus in Iran.

We arrived in the city of Constantine where we settled into our hotel, which had fine views of the lower and more open part of the gorge and some of the bridges across, and had lunch before leaving to see the attractions. Our first visit was to the Grand Mosque, a very fine and striking building which with its very tall minarets and dome can be seen from many parts of the city. While the exterior of the building is completely modern the inside of the mosque, with some very much older sections remaining, was also most impressive, added to which there was no restriction on photography.

Granbd Mosque, Constatine.

We were then driven up to the top of the city where the French built Victory Arch has a magnificent view down over the steepest part of the gorge. We were told that the walk down back to the hotel would take about an hour and a half so some of us elected to return to the hotel in the coach. When I set out to explore the lower part of the city, for I hoped to find a good viewpoint looking up the gorge, one of the policemen appeared nd offered to show me round and I had a considerable job to persuade him that I was perfectly capable of finding my own way without any help. Even though I have a strong opinion that he did indeed follow me at a distance. There were certainly several cases where different members of the group found they were being followed when they set out individually. Many of the houses at this lower level were from the 10thg century and very attractive. I eventually found my viewpoint before returning to the hotel. We all had dinner at the hotel that evening since all the cafes and restaurants were closed that evening due to the presidential elections.

Victory Arch, Constantine.

The *gorgen Constantine,with cable car above bridge.*

Friday, our Good Friday, proved to be a perfect day weatherwise with cloudless skies and yet not too hot. We drove, first, to the Roman site of Tiddis. On the way we passed a very shabby roadside café with the name of "Restaurant Cordon Bleu ". Unfortunately there was not a possible stopping place from where we could take photos.

Tiddis itself was, though not on our original itinerary, a lovely hillside site and during the whole of our time there it was only visited by one other small family, despite the large parking area at the bottom. We had to walk up a steep Roman road and through a fine arch to reach the ruins of the main town. The steep road continued with a sheer drop on one side and several dwelling carved into the cliff on the other. When the road eventually flattened out we found the remains of any other houses, baths, arches and temples, as well as quite a number of large stones with letters or pictures carved on them. The occupants of our accompanying escort, of two cars this time, did not join us on this climb but remained relaxing at the bottom. We spent quite a long time at Tiddis before leaving, for what was to prove our main visit of the day, Djemila. This is one of the two largest Roman sites in Algeria and considered by some to be the finest. Timgad, the other huge Roman site we never got to visit because of security worries, although it remained on our itinerary for several days as a possible place to visit. We had a shock at the number of families visiting when we arrived until we remembered that Friday was the equivalent of our Sunday and the place wa so large that the numbers were at no point a worry to us.

Roman site of Tiddis.

After meeting a local guide ,for our own guide was not allowed to lecture to us on this site, we were taken first to the museum which had some more superb mosaics, though once again photography was not allowed , then to the main site which is on a hillside covered with the ruins. We started by seeing the large public baths, still in remarkable condition, before carrying on to visit the Christian area with a fine baptistery and basilicas and then to the forum and several temples, theatre and even a number of mosaics still in situ. We were not herded round together, though our local guide was never far away if we wished to ask questions and our accompanying

Policemen quite often put in an appearance. The visiting families with their footballs and picnics actually added to the atmosphere.,

General view of Djemila.

Djemila views.

Djemila views.

After a long time at Djemila we left for our hotel at Setif where we were to stay for two nights. This hotel, which was not on our original itinerary but which had been arranged overnight to allow for the possibility of visiting Timgad if it was considered safe, was officially rated 3*, though my room certainly was more of a 1* standard with very basic furnishings and an electric plug hanging out of the wall. However six of us decided to stay in the hotel for supper since we had had such a long day and the food and the wine were surprisingly good. We were joined later by two more members of the party who had been unable to find a recommended café.. Three more when they eventually returned said they had found somewhere to eat but that it had been revolting. When our bill arrived we found that they had charged us a lot too little and the staff refused to correct their mistake although we did try our hardest to be honest.

We discovered during the course of the meal that the American lady in our group had been in Egypt at the time of the Arab Spring uprising and also, recently, in a Japanese earthquake ! We also discovered that the Algerian President had been re-elected by a large majority despite the fact that his health was so bad thast he could hardly lift up his arm to put his voting slip in the ballot box. However we would not be going to Timgad the next day since it was still closed due to the danger of possible violence in that area.

The whole of the next day was spent in exploring Setif which proved to be a remarkably interesting town. We started by walking to the nearby museum which

Dionysus being towed in a chariot pulled by two tigers and the procession included not merely people but also many other animals among which were an elephant and a giraffe. We were told that this was the only Roman mosaic in existence which displays a giraffe.

Roman mosaic of Dionysus, Setif.

After a long visit to the museum we walked down to the centre of the town past an extraordinary modern statue on a roundabout. Here we found an archaeological garden where many of the Roman artefacts were displayed. After a time Erwin said we should either find somewhere for lunch or return to the hotel. Feisal was obviously worried by this splitting up of the party and when he caught me up tried to persuade me to join a group he had collected together for lunch. It took me some time to convince him that I was capable of managing by myself and I eventually found a café called "Happy Bunny" where I was able to eat at leisure before returning to the hotel. I was told later that we were the first group accompanied by Fiesal which did not keep together as one body and I think he disapproved of Erwin for giving us so much individual freedom.

Rounbdabout, Setif.

Archaeological Garden, Setif.

Later that afternoon we walked out again through a well furnished children's playground to the fine remaining city walls stopping on the way to partake of some excellent ice cream. We also discovered that the hotel had an aviary in the grounds

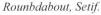

86

where several large and smaller exotic birds including Peacocks, Peahens, Ostriches, Parakeets, Ducks and Geese were kept in one large roofless compound. That had obviously had their wings clipped for they made no effort to escape after the wild birds who frequently visited, probably for the food they were given. We also heard that the final hopes for a visit to Timgad had disappeared but that a visit to a different Unesco site called Madaure had been arranged instead.

The next day, Sunday, we made an impressive exit from Setif to go to Madaure. We were led by a gendarmerie car followed by a local police car. Then came our coach followed in turn by a very large black limousine containing the sub-prefect of the Province, four Unesco officials who were guardians of the site, a senior army officer and an official photographer. This was followed in turn by another police car and, finally by another gendarmerie car. I must add that each of the police and gendarmerie cars contained four armed men. When we finally reached Madaure we stopped by the town hall where the inhabitants of the limousine descended and stood in a line to shake our hands as we passed them. When I reached the army officer he suddenly stood to attention and saluted me before shaking hands. I still can not think why. We were then taken into a room where we were given bottles of water and light refreshments. We were also told that had they had earlier warning of our arrival we would have been given a proper lunch. After the meeting we were driven to the nearby Roman forum with its ruined buildings standing below some weirdly shaped stratified cliffs, obviously shaped in some earthquake, where we had our picnic lunch, under the watchful eyes of numerous armed police, before walking round the ruins themselves. We were told that there were numerous other Roman sites further up in the hills but that we could not visit them. The important officials had departed after the meeting and we did not see them again.

Roman ruins at Madaure.

Immediately below the ruins there lay the remains of what once have been a huge mosque with only the very tall minaret standing in its entirety. A few of our party actually climbed up inside but most of us contented ourselves with wandering around the remains before we were all taken to a small local museum which appeared to have been opened just for our visit. It was at this point the gendarmerie departed leaving us with just two police cars.

Mosque minaret, Madaure,   Madaure museum.

We now had a long drive to our next hotel situated near to Algiers airport for it had now been decided that the next day we were to taske the very long motorway drive to Oran, a large port in the far west of the country not far from the border to Morocco. We were told that if anyone did not wish to do this arrangements would be made to fly them directly back to Britain. No one took advantage of this offer despite the fact that the local news that evening announced that an army patrol in the mountains near Timgad had just been ambushed by terrorists and twelve of them had been killed.

We had to leave early for Iran since the distance, even by motorway, was well over four hundred kilometres. After some distance we arrived at a provincial boundary with no police car waiting to mtake over from our escort. After a short wait and some telephone calls the police said it would be safe for us to go to Oran without escort, so we carried on with only one further stop at a French style motorway services area. In Oran itself there was so much traffic that we missed having the police leading us. However we eventually found our hotel, the Timgad, in the centre of the city near the main square and with, from my room, a good view to the castle overlooking the port. There was no official parking at the hotel but the traffic police working at the busy crossroads allowed the coach to park, partly on the pavement, almost touching the walls of the building which allowed other traffic to move normally but must have made life very difficult for pedestrians. After settling in several of us found a café where we had a good lunch before setting out, with police escort, to visit the castle area. First we visited the attractive Spanish church and then, since the castle was closed due to restoration work, drove to the highest point above the city with very fine views over the port.

On our return we disembarked from the coach in the main square and walked to visit the theatre, very much in the French style, both inside and out, though showing signs of wear. After this we walked past our hotel to visit what had been the cathedral but had now been changed into the city library. Inside there was an artist busy drawing a picture of "Jealously". We ended the day together in the same café where we were able to get a good supper and where we once again had to be photographed for publicity purposes.

View from my Iran hotel room.

Oran. The Spanish Church.

Oran. The theatre.

Oran. The library converted from Cathedral.

The next day started very cloudy and it threatened rain as we set off, but the clouds soon cleared and the weather became lovely. We drove, accompanied by an escort of two police cars, south, away from the coast to a place called Tlemen, a very attractive town with a lovely main square. On the way we had a stop at a modern memorial to Amir Abdel Kader a local hero who had first divided the area between himself and the French but had later rebelled in 1839 and for a time controlled two thirds of Algeria. However by 1847 he was forced to surrender and was imprisoned in France. He was later freed by Louis Napoleon and was sent by the French to Damascus where he intervened in an attack on Christians, saving 12,000 of them including the French consul and staff. He was now honoured by the French but, although he could have returned to Algeria, he retired from all public life and continued to live in Damascus until his death in 1883. We also took a comfort stop in a small town with yet another most unusual roundabout decoration.

When we reached Tlemen we met with a guide who had been recommended to us by one of our party who had met him in Algiers. He first took us round a small museum in the square where the modern age had been adopted for it had very many virtual exhibits and it was a real hands on experience. We were next taken to another building in the square which had once been a mosque and then converted by the French into a wine bar and was now an attractive small museum. One side of the square was taken up by an active mosque and we were told that non muslims were only allowed to enter it if arrangements had been made a ful week in advance, but that negotiations were being carried out to see if we could visit it the next day.

Memorial to Amir Abdel Kader.   *Another unusual Algerianroundabout.*

1.
2.   *Tlemen main square.*   *MUSEUM IN Tlemen.*

We were dropped for lunch at an extremely good restaurant while Erwin and Feisal. With our passports, went on to deal with booking in facilities at the Ibis Hotel where it had been arranged we would be spending the night. When after lunch we were taken to the hotel we found Erwin in a state of great frustration and annoyance for the hotel had insisted that it could not book us in until we had each individually filled in another form similar to that we had to complete before landing in the country. All this took a long time so it was lucky that the hotel proved to be the most comfortable of the entire *trip.*

Later in the afternoon we were taken uphill first to see the remains of Mansourah an old palace which had recently been restored and was built into the city walls, and then to the ruins of an immense mosque and a huge minaret, the only part still not a ruin. This minaret was of such a size that it was said the imam had had a white horse which he used to ride up to the top when he had to call the muezzin. As a memory of that time a white horse is still kept tethered at the entrance.

Next we erer transported, some by cable car and some by the coach, to the top of a cliff where stood the Renaissance Hotel with wonderful views down over Tlemen

After which the coach took us all back to the Ibis for supper.

Restored remains near Tlemen,   *Minaret of mosque.*

The next day was to prove equally fine and interesting. We first drove into the centre of Tlemen where we stopped and waited for a long period nearby to find whether we had been granted permission to visit the Grand Mosque. Eventually word came through that permission had been granted. It proved well worth the wait, even though photography was not allowed. The mosque had been built in 1083 and inside was similar to the Great Mosque at Cordoba in Spain and even though it was not quite as large it showed what Cordoba would have looked like before the Christian church was built inside

We next drove quite a distance to see some caves which for the colour and size of the stalactites and stalagmites were as fine as any I have ever seen. On the return we stopped by an attractive waterfall and pool, some way above which was an iron railway bridge which had been built by Eiffel, famous for his tower in Paris. Unfortunately this was too far away to be worth photographing.

When we returned to Tlemen we drove next to Sidi Boumedienne on a hill just outside the city. This was where the Ottoman attackers had built a palace and mosque during their third and finally successful seige of Tlemen. This was a remarkable complex considering that it was built so speedily during the seige and seems far more like an attractive and permament building with its marvellous views over the city. The main doorway reminded me of a building in Iran for there were two door knockers of different sizes, one on each side of the double doors. These gave out a different noise when used and one was for men and the other for women and children so that the person admitting visitors would know the sex of the person seeking admittance.

Sidi Bomedienne. Tlemen.

We were given plenty of time to explore the well restored palace, mosque and medressa before returning to the centre of Tlemen where we had a late lunch and then time to explore the city. Three of us who went together much of the time had fun watching the policeman who followed us wherever we went. What he did towards the end when we split up to go in different directions I do not know since I did noit see him again. We finally met together for the journey back to Oran where most of us found ourselves in the same rooms as before.

On Thursday we left punctually for the long trip back to Algiers. On the approach to the city there was a several miles long traffic jam in the opposite lane. When we ourselves hit the traffic our accompanying police car displayed its blue lights and put on its siren to make other cars get out of the way so we reached our hotel in good time for lunch. In fact on this journey our new police cars were waiting for us at each of the five changes and all of them led us without stopping straight through each of the seven road blocks on the journey.

After booking in and a quick lunch we were taken, in the coach, up the hill to the top of the Casbash from where we had a fine view of the city. I gathered from my guide book that until recently it had been considered a dangerous area and that anyone visiting had to be accompanied by a policeman. Matters had now considerably improved though we had to wait quite a time before a local guide appeared to take us down on foot. We started by visiting two recently restored merchant's houses and then followed the guide down the steep narrow streets where there was much restoration of buildings, including some from Roman times, taking place. Towards the bottom we visited the Museum of Ceramics and Calligraphy which, though not large, was housed in a fine building and had some excellent exhibits on show.

When we finally reached the bottom, not far from our hotel, we took to our coach again, though this time there was no police escort, to go and see the cathedral. Unfortunately we soon found ourselves in a solid traffic jam and after moving only about a hundred yards in half an hour it became obvious that we would not reach the building before it closed for the evening so we all dismounted and walked back to the hotel, leaving our poor driver to extricate himself as best he could. After supper we met on the terrace, with its fine night time views, for drinks and a chat.

Algiers. Restored house in the Casbah.

Algiers. Museum of Ceramics and Calligraphy.

It rained heavily during the night and the heave clouds we woke to suggested there might be quite a lot of rain to come. However during breakfast the skies cleared during breakfast and it was sunny as we drove westward along the coast to visit a huge mausoleum to some unknown person but know as the Tomb of the Christian which was visible from some miles away.

The Tomb of the Christian.

View from the Tomb of the Christian.

We next drove on to the town of Chechell which, with some Roman columns, claims to have the most beautiful square in Alferia, though personally I preferred the square at Tlemen which we had seen so recently. We stopped at the museum which is on one side of the square. Once again there were some fine mosaics as well as many other artefacts. Unfortunately photography was, as so often, forbidden.and there were no good postcards.

When we came out from the museum we found that the weather had changed again and that it was now raining. Since we were given time to explore the majority of us who had brought umbrellas retrieved them from the coach. Chechel proved to be an interesting place with many scattered remains in different parts of the town so we were able to visit the ruins of baths, temples, arches and an amphitheatre before buying suitable food for a picnic lunch.

Hechel.. Square and museum.

Chechel. Roman arch.

By the time we had returned to the coach the rain had stopped and on the way to the Roman seaside sit at Tipasa we were able to make a stop to see the Roman acqueduct. Indeed when we reached Tipasa the clouds had cleared and it remained ver sunny for the rest of the day. The entrance to the site took us immediately to the Forum and here we sat to eat our picnic lunch while waiting for the local guide, for this was one of the places where only the local guides were allowed to perform, though one was allowed to wander at will. The guide, when he did arrive, proved to be both interesting and knowledgeable and took us to many places we might have missed had he not been there. However we did also have plenty of time to explore by ourselves. The site was crowded since it was a Friday and was in easy reach of Algiers but was so large that visitors were not a worry and its position on the seaside, nestling among the many trees, was delightful and made this one of our best visits. Incidentally once again we appeared to be the only foreigners there.

We were able to see the ruins of numerous temples, theatres, baths, necropolis and Christian churches with their mosaic floors still in situ. Two small dead trees had also been carved into modern sculptures by a local artist.

After leaving the site we walked down the road to visit the local museum which, though small, once again housed some marvellous Roman mosaics. Indeed I think the standard of mosaics in Algeria are every bit as high as those in Tunisia and Libya though there may be fewer of them and there is no mosaic museum to match those of the Bardo and El Djem in Tunisia.

On our return to Algiers we told our new police escort as we entered the city that we wished to go and see the Cathedral. The police said "NO" since there was a football match nearby and they feared there might be violence. Our own guide objected so strongly that we feared he might be arrested. We were eventually able to persuade him that he had not let us down and that no one could have done more.

However he did say that it might still be possible to visit before leaving for the airport the next morning.

Tipasa. Ruins of the Roman City.

On our final morning some of the party decided to sleep in late but the majority of us boarded the coach in a final attempt to see the French Cathedral of Notre Dame d'Afrique even though we had been told we would probably only be able to see the exterior since it was not due to open until we would have to leave for the airport. The building was high upon another of the hills overlooking the city and the view from it was remarkable. Also we were lucky for though the cathedral was still closed the arrival of our coach was noted and the priest in charge appeared and unlocked the building for us. He also said we might photograph inside despite many notices saying photography was forbidden. This fine church was built in the middle of the 19th. Century and had recently been restored. The priest told us that there were many visitors of whom a very large majority were Muslims.

I was particularly impressed by the painting in the apse under which was painted jn large words "Notre Dame de L'Afrique. Priez pour nous et pour les Musulmens". I was also interested to see that all the representations of Our Lady, whether painting or statue, showed her as a black person. I gathered that the Cathedral was under police protection for twenty four hours a day, even though there had never been any trouble. This was the final visit of our trip before an uneventful flight home. Shortly after our return it was reported that a French lone tourist had been kidnapped and executed by terrorists so perhaps the police guard had been necessary.

Algiers. Cathedral of Notre Dame de L'Afrique.

Algiers. Apse of Cathedral of Notre Dame de L'Afrique.

Chapter Five

Eastern Bulgaria and its Thracian Treasures.

A typical church in Nesebur..

When I had been visiting Bulgaria in 2013 my excellent guide, George, had said that I ought to visit Eastern Bulgaria which was, in the main, far less known and that there were many places of interest that he was sure I would find interesting. He also suggested that I should visit Ukraine. I took his advice but unfortunately the visit I arranged to Ukraine had to be cancelled due to the Russian invasion. However Bath Travel and Regent holidays managed to get George to arrange an itinerary for me in Eastern Bulgaria and to find a time when he would once again be able to be my guide.

My plane out was met by another member of the Bulgarian firm who were the local agents, for George was finishing off another tour that day. My hotel was different but was in a good position even nearer to the excellent restaurant I had used the previous year.

After settling in my room I walked to the city centre and found that the Lion Bridge was closed for there was much work being done and there was now a tunnel under the waterway which also connected with the underground station and emerged just by the hotel of my previous visit. I visited, once again, the Memorial Cathedral and bought an icon from a stall just nearby. The Archaeological Museum was unfortunately closed though I hoped that I might have time to visit it at the end of my trip. In the evening I had another very good supper in the nearby restaurant and was surprised that I was remembered from my visit the previous year.

Covered Bazaar, Sofia.   *Restaurant, Sofia.*

The next morning George arrived with his car and we set out for a long drive, past Plovdiv for our first visit which was to see the remains of the mountain top Thracian city of Perperikon. The Regent Holiday instructions gave warning of a steep climb to the top which was "quite challenging" I had been a little worried by this especially since my guide books which mention it also stress the difficulty of getting to the top. However in the event the path up which George led me was not too steep and I managed it quite easily, though the route by which we descended would have been more difficult if we had reversed our journey. The weather which had seemed unsettled when we started had by now turned into a misty drizzle but that had the advantage it was not too hot and even the drizzle had stopped by the time we reached the top.

This place is remarkable and yet outside Bulgaria it seems to be hardly known. One of my three guide books just mentioned it in one sentence, while the others gave it little greater attention, and even in Bulgaria there were very few visitors when we were there, though there were half a dozen stalls down at the not very large car park selling tourist trivia suggesting that it might get the occasional coach. There is evidence of human residence dating from about 6000 BC and lasting until the 14th Century AD when it was destroyed by invaders. Religious practices seem to have been introduced in the early Iron Age. On the Acropolis a very large temple, thought to have been dedicated to Dionysus. Had been converted into a church in the 4th to 5th centuries. There are many places carved into the rocks where there is evidence that gifts for the gods were left. There are the ruins of a huge two storey palace covering about 1700 square metres, with over fifty rooms, some of them also .carved into the rocks. Many remains of paved roads still in good condition make for easy walking around the large number of ruined houses once the top level has been reached. The whole of the city was surrounded by a wall, parts of which still exist, though it would have seemed to be a natural stronghold on its own with just two entrance arches. Another reason possible for its lengthy existence is the fact that there used to be a gold mine only two kilometres away.

Our next visit, a few miles away, was to the hill top Sanctuary dating from the 12th century BC including the Tatul Tomb which is believed to have been dedicated to the famous singer Orpheus. The whole structure, with its surrounding walls is visible from a long distance and the walk to it from a neighbouring hamlet was down a path through trees and sweet smelling vegetation. Once again this seems little known and this time there were not even any buildings nearby except for an entrance kiosk where the ticket seller appeared surprised to see any visitors.

Perperikon.

Perperikon

Perperikon   *Tomb of Orpheus, Tatul.*

After a good night's sleep in the town of Kardzhali we set off the next morning in fine sunny weather. This was to be an interesting day for George himself had not been to most of the places we were to visit, though they were places he had long wanted to see for he had heard many things about them. Our first stop was to be at the remarkable Thracian tomb of Alexandrovo, dating back to the 4th century BC. This was only discovered in the year 2,000AD. It was decided that it would not be possible to open the tomb to the public so a remarkable building was built nearby with the help of a grant of nearly three million dollars by Japan. This building, opened in 2009, holds not only some of the finds from the tomb but also an exact replica of the tomb itself with its extraordinary frescos. One can see the original mound standing among trees at a little distance. It is lucky that the tomb still exists for many of the Thracian tombs have been, in the past, broken into and their valuable contents stolen and frescos often destroyed, by treasure seekers. The size of the entrance is so narrow that it would have been impossible to fit even a small group in at one time and some of the frescos would soon have been damaged by people rubbing against them.

As it was there were very few other visitors and I was able to spend plenty of time seeing everything. I gathered that when there were more visitors viewing time was strictly limited, though there were also large copies of the frescos hanging from the walls, but these did still not give the same impression as that gained by standing in the tomb replica itself.

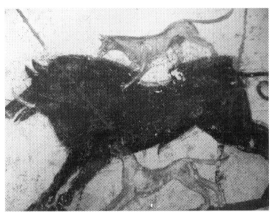

Frescos in the Alexandrovo Tomb.

We next carried on to the town of Nova Zagoro, and after some difficulty in finding the way due to a peculiar one way system we eventually reached the museum only to find it had just shut for a long lunch break. In view of this we drove 10 Kms out of the town to see the Karanova Mound which covers areas dating from Neolithic to the Bronze Ages. This is one of the largest and oldest settlement mounds in Bulgaria, or, according to one Internet entry, in Europe. Excavations have discovered no less than seven cultural layers but there is little to be seen now except for a notice board, rather worn, with some pictures of the many objects found in each layer and a huge measuring stick showing where each level was.

Karanova Settlement Mound.

When we arrived it was firmly locked although it was officially open. However after a telephone call and a twenty minute wait the man responsible arrived on a bicycle. I should imagine the number of visitors is negligible for the excavators have left little to be seen by anyone who was not an expert archaeologist so we did not spend a very long time there though I had plenty of opportunity to walk among the overgrown weeds and see what remained to be seen.

On returning to Nova Zagora we had lunch before going to see the museum which was now open. This was a rewarding visit for thousands, one Internet entry says 40,000, of the finds of the Karanova Mound are on display though no photography was allowed. What I did find extraordinary was the fact that none of my three Bulgarian guide books even mentioned this excellent museum.

We next drove on to Burgas, an attractive city on the Black Sea coast. After booking in to the hotel I took a walk to see the excellent, and not overcrowded, beach and part of the city which has many fine 19th century buildings.

The "Crowded" ! Burgas beach.

Burgas railway station.

The next morning we first went to the much more visited coastal town of Nesebur. This was to prove quite the most crowded place in my trip for it is near to the very popular resort of Sunny Beach and is the great place of visit for the holiday makers there. However despite all the tourists it was still worth visiting. It is a small town of some 11,000 inhabitants situated on what used to be an island but is now joined to the mainland by a man made causeway. It is one of the oldest settlements in Europe, dating from Thracian times and is recognised as a World Heritage site. Despite its small size it is still possible to get away from the most touristified areas and is full of delightful cottages and the remains of some forty churches dating from the 5th to the 17th centuries, several of them still in good condition, in the most attractive local style of white stone alternating with red brick frequently, further decorated with ceramic discs, blind arcading and fine roof tiles. Some of them, in particular the 11th century New Metropolitan Church, have very fine frescos inside.

Typical Nesebur Church.

Frescos in the New Metropolitan Church, Nesebur.

I found a pleasant little open air restaurant with good views of the sea and which was not crowded where I stopped for my lunch. There were lovely flowers in the garden and just across a narrow road were a mother and her daughter, aged about ten, both busy doing oil paintings of the view. I got the impression that the girl was in fact a better painter than her mother.

City walls of Nesebur.

Modern statue in Nesebur

Typical Nesebur street.

George, who had led me into the centre of the town gave me a long time to explore by myself and it was a very enjoyable visit.

We next left for Varna, the largest Bulgarian city on the Black Sea coast where our hotel, the Odessos proved to be in an excellent position at the entrance to an attractive park where there was a delightful little children's train and not far from the sea. It was interesting that despite its size and many fine 19th and early 20th century buildings there were very few foreign tourists there. Next door to the hotel there was a huge very modern building which proved to be a bookshop. Unfortunately, despite its size, there were practically no books in English about the country. The next morning we visited the 19th century cathedral where the local Archbishop was conducting the service with a very fine male choir. There are, apparently only three Archbishops in Bulgaria and I have now seen two of them.

Children's train, Varna.

Varna cathedral..

We also visited the Archaeological Museum where are exhibited some wonderful golden artefacts, claimed to be the oldest worked gold in the world, from about 4,000BC, which were discovered in 1972 and excavated from the Varna Chalcolithic Necropolis. There are some two thousand of these golden objects made of nearly pure 23.5 carat gold. It was extraordinary to me that the Museum was nearly empty since it had such incredible exhibits. Unfortunately photography was forbidden and I could find no postcards.

When we left Varna we drove a short distance to the stone forest of Pobiti Kamani. This, though hardly mentioned in my English guide books, is one of the most remarkable natural formations I have ever seen. It is about 50 sq kilometres and consists of natural standing stones, many of them apparently hollow. They are evidently many millions of years old and there are several theories about how they were formed.

Stone forest of Pobiti Kamani.

It is supposed to be unique in the world and the part of it that we saw has been designated as a Heritage site. There were a few families visiting when we were there but no signs of any coaches, or for that matter room for any that did come to park.

We next continued to Pliska, which was the first capital of the Kingdom of Bulgaria between 681 and 1014 during which time it became a Christian country in 865. When it ceased to be the capital it was deserted and little remains to be seen except for the city walls and the ruins of a large church as well as the foundations of many buildings and the remains of a water supply, a sewerage system and a reservoir which were uncovered during archaeological excavations. The amount that remains to be excavated is huge. What has been done was done under the control of the archaeologist who was responsible for the museum at Varna, and whose tomb is here in Pliska. There is a good little museum which contains models of what the city must have looked like, as well as showing many of the tools recovered and an unusual bronze rosette.

Pliska bronze rosette   *City walls, Pliska.*   *Church, Pliska*

Our next visit was to see the carved horseman of Madara. It was quite a climb up a narrow path before we came to the view point for the carved hunter in the cliff face which despite considerably erosion is still a remarkable sight and very well worth the climb. The horseman himself appears to be carrying a wine vessel in his hand and to judge by the dog with him would seem to be hunting. Once again the few visitors were all Bulgarian except for me.

Madara Horseman.

After this visit we drove to a little village and down an unmade up track to a small hotel known to George. If I ever wanted a holiday doing nothing I might well chose this place for the atmosphere, the garden, the small swimming pool, the natural food and the warmth of our greeting was remarkable

While we were there, a small Russian women's choir arrived for lunch and entertained us, before they ate, with several minutes of marvellous singing. Seldom have I seen people so obviously enjoying their singing as was this choir.

We next drove on to Shumen, a town surrounded on three sides by a steep hill with a huge monument on the top overlooking the whole place and surrounding area. The hotel where I should have stayed was closed for some reason, so George had booked me into an old guest house where I had a large living room next to the bedroom. One of the comfy armchairs was occupied by the largest Teddy Bear I have ever seen. The accommodation in general was very simple and basic but had the great virtue of being clean.

We had been scheduled to go and see the monument but it was closed for the afternoon since it was said to be too windy to be safe. When I had settled in I walked out to visit the local mosque, the largest in the Balkans. This was open, though covered in scaffolding for repairs which have, I gathered, been going on for some ten years and no one knows when the work is likely to be finished. While I was 98 sitting down outside putting on my shoes I suddenly heard a voice with a broad Yorkshire accent say "Can I help you ?" I looked up and discovered a very nice black lady smiling down at me. She was apparently, like me, doing a tour of the area with a guide. She still lived in York where she had been taken as a small child from the West Indies and, like me, was enjoying her trip very much though she was not staying in Shumen. She asked if I had visited the monument on the hill top and I told her that I was being taken up to see it the next morning if the weather allowed.

The monument, the 1300 Years of Bulgaria Monument, was put up in 1981 to commemorate Bulgaria's existence as Europe's oldest nation-state. We were told that there were 1,500 steps to climb up to it out from Shumen, but luckily there was a good road up which we could drive to a point with a level walk to the monument. I had not realised from below quite how large it was. It is made of concrete and is a mixture of columns, animals and historical figures. The views from it are magnificent and show clearly the old walls that surround the town of Shumen itself.

Mosque at Shumen

1300 Years of Bulgaria Monument.

1300 Years of Bulgaria Monument

We next moved on to a Thracian Tomb complex of some four hundred tombs, of which we saw the most important, a tomb with carved caryatids and more marvellous frescos. Unfortunately no photography was allowed inside so I was only able to take a picture of the exterior, nor were there any decent photos or postcards on sale. There were quite a few visitors here and once again all of them Bulgarian. The guide who showed us round spoke no English. I am sure they could do more to attract tourism to this area for there is so much to see. Only in November 2012 was a great golden treasure discovered in a wooden chest during the course of further excavations. This is now displayed in the Archaeological Museum in Sofia.

Our next visit was to the Ivanovo Monastery situated in a lovely wooded river valley and the trip involved quite a long steep walk, but was well worthwhile. The 12th Century cave building is situated in a cliff and is filled with frescos painted directly onto the rough cave walls. The frescos have remained in remarkably good condition, and I found them very interesting as being of a different style than any others I had seen in the country. We were the only visitors.

Thracian Tomb

Ivanovo Rock Monastery

Ivanovo Rock Monastery.

Ivanovo Rock Monastery.

After this visit we travelled to Ruse and when I had settled into my very comfortable room in the three star Ana Palace Hotel with a view of the Danube I went for a walk through the town. Unfortunately I was not able to get much in the way of views of the Danube for there is no walk by the river itself since buildings and a railway, Bulgaria's first, take up much of the space by the river. However the city, which is often called Little Vienna, has many attractive squares and the houses are frequently of 19th Century Art Nouveau style giving it a pleasant and relaxed feel, even though there was a lot in the way of road works in the pedestrianised area near my hotel, which made the start of the walk less pleasant than the later part. I ended my walk by finding an attractive café overlooking a green park where I had an excellent supper, with, as usual, a glass of the excellent Bulgarian red wine, sharing a table with a Belgian woman who proved to be a superb linguist.

City of Ruse.　　　　　　　　　　　　　　　*City of Ruse.*

It rained during the night but cleared up soon after we left for Sofia where we reached the hotel about lunch time. I walked first to see again the Alexandra Nevesky Memorial Cathedral and next the Archaeological Museum, which was open this time and where I was able to see some of the treasures discovered in the Thracian tombs

Thracian Treasures in the Archaeological Museum, Sofia.

The next day I had a punctual flight back to England to finish yet another successful and most interesting holiday.

Chapter 6.
Morocco. Casablanca to Marrakech.

My flight out, by Royal Air Maroc from Gatwick to Casablanca, was punctual and comfortable. The plane was not full but the food was the worst I had ever met on a flight. My driver, Mohammed, was waiting for me and took me to my hotel, His standard of English was not great, but he ;roved to be an excellent driver which was the most important thing and we were to be met by prearranged English speaking guides at most of the places we visited. The hotel was of a sound standard, despite its somewhat peculiar electronics, though I felt that six pillows was somewhat excessive for my bed. There was also a very good view from my room to the huge modern Hassan II mosque.

View from my hotel room.

The next day started with an excellent breakfast including some of the best dates I have ever eaten. Mohammed arrived with a local guide and drove us first to see the Hassan II mosque, the third largest mosque in the world, and built entirely over water in only six years. It can hold 25,000 worshippers inside the building and another 50,000 in the court outside.

When we arrived I joined a small group with an English speaking female guide to see the inside of the mosque for only special mosque guides are allowed to show people round the interior. I gathered that the roof, which weighs 1,100 tons can be slid open in a few minutes, though we were not shown this in action. She also told us that this was one of only two mosques in the country to admit non Muslims as visitors. It was one of the most impressive buildings that I have ever seen. It was a lengthy tour inside for we saw not only the main hall but also some of the rooms underneath and there was no effort made to hurry us.

Casablanca. Hassan II Mosque.

I spent a long time looking at the mosque and its surrounds before we finally regained the car and set out on a visual tour of Casablanca.

Since it was a Sunday the traffic was light. One of the places we saw was the

111

first Macdonalds café to be built in the city many years before. Less than a year later another building which is still used was built on the opposite side of the road. It was an anti-cholesterol hospital. My guide said it was no coincidence. Casablanca is a modern city with wide boulevards an much greenery. We ended our tour by stopping at the cathedral whose walls consist mainly of stained glass.

Casablanca Cathedral.

We now said goodbye to our guide. He had spoken excellent English and had been a guide for Cheri Blair three times and for Tony Blair once. Our next stop on the way to Fez was at Rabat, the capital of Morocco though less known to most tourists than either Fez or Marrakech. Here there was no guide but we visited first the 12thC Hassan Tower and the nearby Mausoleum dedicated to Mohammed 5, the founder of modern Morocco. There was a mounted guard at the entrance to the complex and other foot guards at and inside the Mausoleum. These stood as still as our own guards at Buckingham Palace, and when the guards were changed the marching and movements could not be faulted, though the style of marching was different to the British style.

Rabat entrance to complex.   *Guard inside Mausoleum.*

While in Rabat we also visited the Oudaya Kasbah with its Andalusian gardens and Chellah Necropolis a much larger area than round the Mausoleum that I had wandered around on my own. So; Mohammed, when he had parked the car, came in to join me to make sure that I saw all the most important parts of the site. Here, despite his limited English he proved himself quite capable as a guide and made sure that I reached the best viewpoints for the Chellah Necropolis and the valley beyond as well as the fine ruins of the Kasbah itself.

Hassan Tower and Mausoleum.   *Rabat, Kasbsh. .*

Rabat. Chellah Necropolis.

While in Rabat we also drove round the gardens of the unoccupied Royal Palace, which looked much lovelier than the building itself, before driving on to Fez where we were to spend three nights. On the way there we had a rather amusing incident when we were waved down by the police who told us that they had been phoned by their colleagues further back to stop a car like ours which had been driving well above the speed limit. Mohammed protested that he had not been driving so fast and when the police phoned back they found that the car concerned had a completely different number plate. At that moment another car absolutely similar to ours appeared and it was stopped while we were sent on with apologies.

When we reached Fez we drove through the new town and Mohammed pointed out to me the hotel in which he would be staying. We finally reached the walls of old Fez and Mohammed was instructed where to park before he led me to the Riad where I would be staying. Riads in Morocco are old houses. usually looking inward over an enclosed garden, which have been turned into hotels, some of them very luxurious. The Riad Salama was in a small street quite a walk from the car park and I was shown to a very comfortable room overlooking a lovely garden and open air restaurant where I had an excellent, though far too large supper. Here I met a recently retired Eneritus English professor who was the only other person eating there that evening.

Views from my room in the Riad Salama..

The next day was hot and very humid with temperatures reaching the mid thirties. Mohammed came and collected me after breakfast and drove me through a little town with a market which spread over the road, making it extremely difficult for any driver, past the Roman remains of Volubilis to see a little mountain top town in the Rid mountains before returning to Volubilis where an English speaking guide was waiting to greet me.

Volubilis is the largest Roman site in Morocco and one of the furthest flung cities of the Roman empire. It is built on the site of an old Berber town whoseinfluence can be seen in the layout and is very well worth a long visit. Despite the size and importance of the place there were only two coaches and a few cars there and the other visitors were seldom to be seen among the many capitals, basilicas and triumphal arches. One can see the remains of some of the oil presses that helped create the areas great wealth. There were also a large number of fine mosaics, still in situ and in remarkably fine condition. These tended to be in the private houses away from the most magnificent of the Roman buildings This may account for the fact that neither of the two coach parties and very few of the other visitors were to be seen looking at them, It was certainly bone of the finerst set of Roiman remains I have ever seen, almost up to the standard of Palmyra when I saw it.

Volubilis.

When we had finished our tour I returnd to Mohamed who drove me to Meknes. We had lunch in a restaurant overlooking the main square and I met my next guide who was dressed in Berber fashion. He spoke good English and first made Mohamed drive us round some of Meknes past the Royal Palace which the king does not live in but has been left empty and when we drove round part of the gardens the only bits of the building we could see were the walls. We then parked near a fine gate in the city walls from where we walked into the old part of the city.

Here we first saw the incredible stables, built by the great Sultan Moulay Ishmael, who ruled from 1672 until 1727, in which twelve thousand horses were kept together with enough food for more than two years. Part of this building is now roofless as the result of an earthquake in 1730 but even there the tall stone walls are standing in entirety.

Next we emerged into the market area opposite the mosque. We had to wait a time for it to be opened. This, according to my guide, was one of the only two mosques in Morocco to admit non Muslims into the building. I had of course seen the other in Casablanca. However I had to correct him politely when he said that these were the only two mosques open to non Muslims in the whole of North Africa and he was startled when I told him I dad visited several mosques in Algeria onlt a few months earlier. He had obviously been misinformed about this and I do not think he will make the same mistake again.

At another good supper that night back mat the riad the Emeritus professor and I were joined by a pleasant couple from California who were also staying there. While we were supping a huge quantity of sparrows descended onto the trees in the garden all singing at the tops of their voices. I have often heard a dawn chorus of birds but this is the only occasion on which I have heard an evening chorus of sparrows.

Meknes. City gate.

Meknes. Sultan Moulay Ishmail stables.

When I drew the curtains next morning it was to see a grey sky with heavy clouds looking like rain. However the clouds soon dispersed and it became very hot and humid. At 9.30 a guide appeared and we set out to see the city only to discover after a few minutes that he was not my guide but was the man intended for the Californian couple. My proper guide appeared just after our return so we set out again. We first paid a visit to the old Koranic school which is meant for the very young pupils who start to learn the Koran by heart.

Next we began to walk up the main street where the shops were only just starting to open. The country changes to summer time as we do here but the shopkeepers do not pat ant attention to this and continue to open whenever they wish. The religious buildings were open however and we visited several of these as well as a school where we saw fine decorative tiling. We also saw an extraordinary ancient water clock with twelve separate wooden water channels each of which made a different noise when opened to tell the hour. How it worked I could not understand.

Fez Koranic school.

Fez. Water clock.

Another school that we saw was most unusual in that it boasted its own minaret. We were not allowed to see inside any of the classrooms here but did enter the courtyard where there was a large pool carved out of one huge piece of marble. We were also able to look into the mosque itself from its courtyard.

After leaving the Souk by the upper gate we found a money exchange shop before returning to the souk and starting down the other main street. All the streets including the main streets are too narrow to take motorised traffic and all goods are delivered by horse, donkey or hand. The shops were now all open and it was noticeable that they were not aimed at the tourist trade. In this it was similar to Aleppo when I had visited it, though that has, I gather, now been destroyed in the Syrian civil war. Among the places we saw was what is reputed to be the oldest university in the world, a very large tannery, an art gallery where I nearly bought a painting, a metal working area and a wood carving museum. For me it was even more interesting than the covered bazaar in Istanbul.

Fez. Marble pool in school yard.

Fez. University.

Fdez. Mosque entrance.

Fez. Metal making area.

Fez. Tannery.

The trip around the souk took several hours and after a light lunch in one of the eating places I made another trip of exploration so that when I finally returned to the riad I was glad to take a rest before another excellent supper in the garden restaurant, once again accompanied by the tremendous noise made by the flocks of sparrows. I have known starlings behave like this before, especially in Turkey, but never sparrows.

The next morning , after a good breakfast, I was collected from the riad by Mohammed, who very kindly insisted on carrying my case to the car. Before finally leaving Fez he drove us up to see the entrance gate to the Royal Palace above the city. The king appeared to own many palaces around Morocco but seemed to use very few of them.

Fez. Breakfast table.

Fez. Royal Palace entrance.

Our journey to Marrakech started by driving a considerable distance along an under construction dual carriageway followed bt climbing steeply up a very winy single track road through bleak and barren countryside into the Mid Atlas mountains until we reached the small town of Ville Difranche in what is called the Green Valley where vegetation was suddenly prevalent. We stopped here for a leg stretch and to photo a lion sculpture in an attractive park before driving on a few miles where we turned off the main road to see the Cedar Forest and a wild monkey sanctuary. The road ended in a clearing in the forest where stood a long dead huge cedar tree. There may well have been other cedars in the forest but we did not see them. There were however many monkeys attracted to the area by the food brought by the visitors.

Lion in Ville Difranche park.　　　　　　　　*Cedar Forest monkeys.*

Monkey with Mohammed.

On our return to the main road we found a café for a lunch stop before driving on to Marrakech where we drove to the edge of the great Fna square where we had to stop the car and were met be one of the riad staff together with the Emeritus Professor who proved to be staying at the same riad and had travelled by train. It was quite a walk to the riad which stood in a maze of narrow alleys on the far side of the square.

The Riad Hayka proved to be every bit as good as the Riad Salama in Fez with excellent rooms all looking out over the lovely enclosed garden where the meals, again first rate, were served.

The next morning I was met by a guide for a tour of Marrakech. He led me to our car which Mohammed had somehow managed to drive onto my side of the Fna square and we drove first to the Koutoubia Minaret and the remains of its mosque complex. The minaret dominates the city and is so large that the muezzin used to ride a horse up inside it to reach the place from which he made the call to prayer.

Marrakech. Koutoubia minaret.   *Marrakech. Taxis stand.*

Next I was taken to see the Saadian Tombs. These were hidden behind some very high walls which were built by an Ottoman sultan who had captured Marrakech and did not like the way the dead were venerated, They were forgotten about and only rediscovered again in 1916.They are now some of the most visited buildings in the city but despite the crowds are well worth seeing for their decorations.

Saadian Tombs. Marrakech.

Saadian Tombs.

Our next visit was to the ruins of the huge El Badi Palace. Little remains of this except for the walls on top of which the storks were nesting. However in one room which was still existing just inside and attached to the walls was an exhibition of photographs from the 1960's by a Moroccan photographer which included a very well known picture of Christine Keeler and another of the Beatles. There were few other visitors here. Outside was a small spice market where we found a little café for an excellent fresh orange juice.

Marrakech. Walls of El Badi Palace.   *El Badi Palace. Room with photographic exhibition.*

We then went to see two much smaller palaces which have now been converted into museums. These had beautiful gardens and the rooms themselves showed the luxurious way in which the rich here lived in the 19th and early 20th centuries.

Marrakech. Palace museums.

Marrakech Palace museum.

Marrakech. Marjorelle garden.

We also visited a fine Jewish house which had been turned into a carpet shop. My itinerary showed that after lunch we would do a tour of the souks but I decided that I would do that by myself later and persuaded my guide to take me to the Marjorelle garden which lies a little outside the walls of the city. This garden, which was later owned by Yves Saint Laurent, is one of my favourite gardens anywhere in the world.

The garden contains over 400 varieties of palm trees and nearly 2,000 species of cactus as well as a great number of brightly coloured tropical and other flowers and plants, including water lilies. The studio built by Marjorelle is painted bright blue and has been converted into a small museum with a selection of modern crafts.

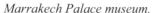

Marrakech. Marjorelle garden.

After I had spent nearly two hours in the garden I was taken back to the entrance mof the Fna Great Square from where I walked to the riad. After a short rest I set out to explore the nearby souks. The shops here were far more geared to the tourist than were those of Fez. However many of them were interesting and I was very interested to see a shop of wooden objects which were being made by a man with his feet. The whole area was extremely lively and colourful. There was more pressure to enter the shops and view the contents but at no time did it become excessive.

Marrakech souk..

Marrakech foot woodworker.

The next day I was picked up by my guide after breakfast and taken to the car which was once again parked in the Fna Gret Square. I found that certain cars were allowed to menter the square early in the morning at the same time as the stalls were being erected but that later in the day no motor traffic, except for police cars and ambulances were permitted. We now drove out of the city and along a dual carriageway towards the Ourika valley in the High Atlas mountains, past olive groves and orchards. Shortly after the dual carriageway finished we turned off the main road and drove to a Berber village in the mountains. This road was so narrow that the driver and guide had both at times to hang out of their windows to watcch the edge of the road. There was certainly no way in which the coach could have made the trip. The village itself was fascinating. The houses were still being buit in the same way as they had been for a thousand years. Electricity had recently been installed and the television discs looked very incongruous on some of the roofs.

. We started by visiting the school where the day was divided into two with the infants being taught in the morning, when we were there, and the secondary children in the afternoon in a different room complete with computers. I saw no sign of any books of any sort in either room. ..

Berber village school infants.

Secondary pupils classroom.

Our next visit was to see the potter at work, sitting on the earth floor with his feet working a wheel in a hole in the floor, the same wheel we ere told, that his father had used seventy years before. The outside kiln was made of earth. We then visited his home of two rooms. One of which was the kitchen and the other which was used for everything else. Here the earth floor was covered with rugs bit otherwise there was no separate furniture at all. I think this was one of the most primitive I have ever visited though all the inhabitants we met were most welcoming.

Berber village potter.

Living and sleeping room of Berber cottage.

Berber village main street.

We spent a long time at this village whose name I never discovered. .before driving back along the track to the main road and on to the Ourika valley. I had driven past this area before on my first visit to Morocco but had not stopped ,there for it had recently been devastated by flash floods. The damage done then had been repaired but it was still a fairly unusual place with many of the cafes only approached by very precarious looking pedestrian only rope bridges with wooden plank flooring. Luckily the place where we stopped for lunch was a modern building on our side of the river and well above road level.

Bridge to Ourika valley café.   *View of Ourika valley from our café.*

We had an excellent lunch here, indeed the food everywhere in Morocco was very good, before returning to Marrakech fairly early in the afternoon. The Fna square was now filling up and I was frequently pestered to take pictures of the entertainers and then to pay for having taken a photograph. I only managed to get rid of one man with a monkey on his shoulder by showing him some of the photographs I had taken in the Cedar forest two days before. I also managed to take a few other photographs without being spotted before I set off into the souks again, for I wanted to get to an area I had seen on a previous visit. This area included the Ben Youssef Medressa, the Koubba Ba'Aydin, the Mourassine . Mosque and the Marrakech Museum.

No non Muslim is allowed into the mosque but it has a very fine minaret. The Koubba Ba'Aydin is the only surviving part of a destroyed mosque and contains an ablution pool but entry is not now allowed though I have seen it in the past.

I next went to the museum. The entry ticket for the building also gave admittance to the Medressa about 100 yards away. I was advised that the Medressa would fairly soon be closing so I went there first. Although this Koranic school was founded in the 14th century it was rebuilt in 1564. This is a magnificently decorated building and seems to be unused except as part of the museum. The museum itself is housed in a late 19th century palace and is laid out in the style of a traditional Moorish house. It does not have many exhibits but is nevertheless very well worth seeing for its superb decoration even though very few tourists had made their way there at the time of my visit.

Marrakech. Bven Youssef Medressa..

Main hall of Marrakech Museum.

I walked back to the Fna Square by a different route and by chance found myself in the Artisans' Market. I was glad to see this for here was an open air market made not for the tourist but mainly for the locals.

Artisans'market,   Marrakech.

Marrakech souk.

By the time I reached the Fna Square some of the stalls were shutting up and a lot of the entertainment was starting., though I did little photography of the snake charmers, bands, conjurers and other entertainers since I did not wish to be pestered for money.

Fna Square, Marrakech in the morning.

I had supper in a little café overlooking the square before returning to the riad and had a good night's sleep ready for my flight back to London.

Chapter Seven

Ethiopia: A Truly Extraordinary Early Christian Country.

A priest in his church.

When a chance to visit Ethiopia came I realised I knew very little about the history of the country. I knew it had adopted Christianity at man early stage. I knew that Italy, under Mussolini, had invaded and seized it in the 1930's and that my wife had, for a short time, been at school in Birmingham, with the daughter of the exiled Emperor Haile Sellasie who had returned to the country after the war, had ruled for a time, then been turned off the throne, but had later regained it. I knew that there were many ancient churches and that the scenery was supposed to br beautiful. I remembered there had been a bad famine a few years earlier. When I started more research I found that most of the few guide books said that the altitude was very high and that elderly people should consult their doctors before going to make sure they could manage the heights. I decided that I had better see my GP for most people would consider me elderly at the age of eighty five. Luckily she said "Go for it" and so I went.

I had chosen to travel in February since the weather in Ethiopia seemed to be good at that time of year. It was also fine for my drive up to Heathrow and I arrived in plenty of time for my flight despite part of the A303 being closed so I had to drive through Bulford which I had not seen since my National Service days in 1948. My flight left on time and I found the man sitting next to me was an animal pharmacist who had worked at Phizer in Sandwich for seventeen years for part of which time my son-in-law had also been there though they had not met each other. The food was not up to much even by airline standards but I did manage to get some sleep before we touched down at Addis Ababa shortly after 6AM.

It took a long time to pass through the airport. There were no less than two checks for Ebola. In one of these we had to stare from a distance at what looked like a camera, though how a photograph could tell if you had the symptoms of the disease I do not know. Next there was a very long wait at passport control before we could collect our luggage. Finally the police had to check each piece of luggage with our passports. When we met our guide we had to wait a long time for one of our members to get his visa for he had ignored instructions to obtain it in the UK, We then had to wait for a missing person who was finally found to be waiting For us at the hotel and who had arrived two days earlier, but no one had thought to tell our guide. Luckily the hotel was good, if o0f a rather dull international type   and we had time to have a short rest and an excellent buffet lunch before setting out to see some of Addis Ababa which though a city of four million people had only started being built in 1887.

Our first visit was to the Holy Trinity Cathedral which was built to commemorate the country's return to independence after the occupation by the Italians. It is a large and imposing building. For me the most interesting part was seeing in the graveyard the grave of Sylvia Pankhurst who spent the last part of her life in Ethiopia and a plaque which read "Here are the past but the living legends". I also found the tomb, inside the cathedral, of Haile Selassie most impressive. This was followed by a visit to the Ethnographical Museum, where I discovered, on the top floor, an exhibition of icons which seemed at first sight to be very crude but mat the same time very moving. There was also an interesting display of the different types of musical instruments used in their church services. Our final visit was to the National Museum, where for me the most interesting exhibit was the skeleton on a lady now called Lucy who at 3.1 million years old is the earliest human being ever discovered.

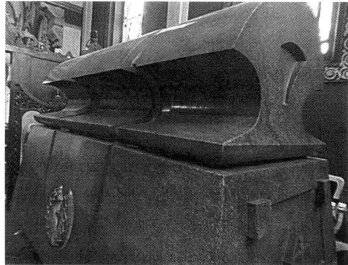

Addis Ababa; Holy Trinity Cathedral.
Tomb of the Emperor Haile Selassie.

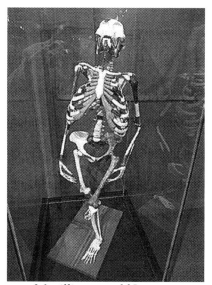

Icon in Ethnographical Museum.
3.1 million year old Lucy.

We all went to bed early since we were all to be woken at 4.45 AM the next morning so we could catch our early morning flight to Mekele.

The security for this internal flight was tremendous. As well as another Ebola check we had to pass through two sets of x-ray machines. However the flight was on time and we arrived at 8.15 AM at Mekele airport. We were seated in our coach very quickly for there were no checks at all and the luggage was unloaded speedily. The coach itself was quite comfortable, though our cases had to be loaded into the back through one of the windows. Indeed this was to happen with each of our coaches.

The weather was lovely with not a cloud in the sky. And it was pleasantly warm but not too hot. The drive toMekele was to give me the first glimpse of the real Ethiopia. To tell the truth I had been slightly disappointed with our firs day in Addis Ababa. We had seen some interesting things but the overall impression was not of something special. Now we were out in the country it was as though we had gone back to the Middle Ages The people we saw by the roadside were no longer dressed in western clothes. The main means of transport seemed to be the donkey. Mekele when we reached it had a number of modern houses but we drove straight to the market and parked where the tarmac came to an end. All the earthen very narrow streets were covered with litter. All the roofs of the shops were made of corrugated iron, most of them very rusty. The walls were made of any available material from mud to plywood and all were single storey. They were obviously not expecting tourists for everything on sale was just for locals. It was a large market but the only motorised vehicle I saw was a rusty lorry laden with objects from China.

Mekele market.

We left Mekele to go to Wukro rock hewn church, but on the way, we discovered that a large cycle race was about to come past travelling in the other direction. We parked our coach off the road near a couple of old lorries, the only other vehicles there and waited for a short time for the race to pass by. We never discovered if it was an international or a national race, but the crowd was very vociferous. At the end we gave a lift to several mothers with babies on their backs since we learnt that otherwise they would have had to wait for several hours for a bus to the next town several miles away.

Some of those to whom we gave a lift after the cycle race.

Our next stop was at the little town called Wukro which is half Muslim and halh Christian. We turned off the not very good tarmac road onto a rough track which led us to the hill on which the church stands. This was the first rock church that I had ever seen. It was by no means a cave church for the whole building was carved out of a cliff, walls, roof and all, though this particular church was like an end of terrace house in that the back wall was still attached to the cliff.

Wukro Chirco rock hewn church.

The bell for Wukro Chirco church.

Some sort of service was taking place when we arrived so we had to wait outside and spent some of the time walking round and up the cliff to the top of the church where we saw the roof and on the way down saw several small buildings connected with the church. When we reached the front of the church again the service was over and we were able to enter. The church is believed by the locals to date from the 4th century but is thought by some experts to have been excavated at a later date probably 10th century and the lovely line drawings on the ceiling certainly date back to at least the 15th century and possibly earlier. The priest had remained in the church for our visit and 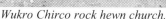 the services.

Inside Wukro Chircos church with priest.   *Our guide by an outbuilding.*

We had lunch at a small café in Wukro before driving on to Abraha Atsbeha, another rock hewn church with very fine frescos. This church, built in the 10th century, but with a large modern porch, is dedicated to two kings of Axum who introduced Christianity into the country in the 4th century and is a great place of pilgrimage for Ethiopians. The frescos date from the 17th century. As we approached the hill where this building stands we passed a large number of women dressed in white ciming from a christening ceremony. When we entered the church we found the priest was still there accompanied by several other men dressed in robes and tall pointed hats who we gathered were priests under training.

Abraha Atsbeha church

Inside Abraha Atsbeha   church.

Our drive now took us through lovely mountain scenery to the next hotel. On the way we stopped to look at the most primitive way of winnowing out grain that I have ever seen. Five oxen were being driven round in circles over the crop, the weight of the hooves separating the wheat from the chaff. Everything would then be thrown up un the air by forks allowing the grain to fall down and the chaff to be blown away.

Our next hotel, the Gheralta Lodge, was in a lovely hill top position with views out to mountains where, we were told, over eighty old rock hewn churches still exist, more than half of them still in use. The hotel itself was thatched and the bedrooms were in two roomed building standing some way from the reception and dining room. Apparently George Bush Junior had stayed in the hotel exactly a year before. My room proved to be the one the ex president had occupied and the other half of the building had been used by one of his entourage. All the rooms had exactly the same fittings and were very comfortable. Before dinner we were given, on the house, an interesting drink of honey wine

Oxen winnowing the crop.   *My room at Gheralta Lodge.*

View from my room.   *Weaver bird and nest outside dining room.*

I would have liked a second night at this place and spent the day exploring the mountains and looking at some of the many churches there, but our tour did not allow for this and we set out for the town of Axum. We were delayed at the start as one of our party was unwell and a taxi had to be arranged to take her straight to Axum since we were due to have several stops on what was supposed to be one of the most winding roads in Ethiopia. The road in places had a rough tarmac surface and there were many roadworks. These so called improvements were being done by Chinese who were supposed to be serving prison sentences in China and had been sent here as unpaid labourers. There work was not of a high standard and the remaining earth roads often gave a smoother drive.

We finally reached a superior road in a small town where we stopped for a time to visit a corn grinding place which was very dark and crowded. This was worked by elderly looking machines. We gathered that many of the poorer villagers paid for the work done not with money but by leaving a portion of the corn with the owners of the machine.

Our next stop was to visit a typical house out in the country. We had to walk over a couple of fields to reach it. The building consisted of two large rooms under a corrugated iron roof. We had to walk through the first room which proved to be a stable holding the family livestock, including cattle, sheep. Hens and cats, in order to reach the room in which the family loved, cooked and slept. The earth floor was covered with a few branches from some shrub scattered around and the only light came from a small hole in the wall for there was no electricity. There were no chairs so we sat on a ledge in the wall which stretched the full length of the room. And there was one large bed in the corner. The whole place was far more primitive than the Berber village I had visited in Morocco. Here we were given coffee. The whole process, which we found repeated several times during our visit to Ethiopia, took over half an hour but the coffee drink produced was delicious. In fact the coffee we had several times during our trip was the finest I have ever tasted anywhere in the world. When heated over a tiny charcoal fire on the floor the beans were ground by hand with a pestle and mortar. Then a wire plate was heated over the same fire and the ground coffee, after we had all sniffed the aroma, was added for further heating.

The first room, (stable in the house).

Coffee making in the other room.

Our next stop was unexpected and unplanned. We came up behind hundreds of women clad in white, men, some of the in soldiers uniform, and schoolchildren waving flags walking along the side of the road and then turning off down onto a large flat area where several big circles of people were already gathered, some of them with drums, starting to make music and to dance. Our coach stopped so that we could see what was going on and when we descended we found that it was celebrating the fourteenth anniversary of the rising of the Tigran Province which had started here and which had led to the fall of the army dictatorship that had seized power from Haile Selassie. We were welcomed to join on the celebrations and spent quite a long tome among the crowds, by now numbering well over two thousand, divided into circular groups. It was interesting that most of these people had arrived on foot some having walked for miles to reach here. The nearest town, from which some had come was well over five miles away and other villages were considerably further afield. There were very few motor vehicles visible.. Each circle appeared to be participating in different activities, the armed men were drilling, some were dancing and most of the children were singing what I took to be patriotic songs. We left reluctantly but we still had a considerable distance to travel and drove off to the town where we were booked for a lunch stop. Then we entered the long winding road which rose up steeply from a height of 2,200 m to one of 3,600 m. We then carried on for a long way, stopping occasionally to look at the marvellous views, and to see from a distance the cliff where the earliest Ethiopian monastery stands and where the monks still have to be pulled up to the building by rope.

For our next visit we departed from the main road and travelled several miles down a dusty track to the village of Yeha where stands the ruins of a 2,500 year old temple the outer walls of which are still standing 8 metres high, made of large rectangular stones without any mortar, though temporarily covered by scaffolding on the inside. What religion was originally practised here is not known, but in the early sixth century it became a Christian monastery.

Travel to Tigran Uprising Anniversary.   *Femple at Yeha.*

Next to this building is a new church with old stone carvings of ibises inserted in the front walls. Finally we went to a little house where we climbed up a steep narrow wooden staircase to a very small room which proved to be crammed full of old church relics including many old illuminated manuscripts, stone carvings and gold crowns.

Church museum at Yeha.

This museum boasts, probably truthfully, to be one of the most remarkable treasure houses of any Ethiopian church. It was certainly by a long way the smallest museum I have ever seen. At no tome could we fit more than four of our group plus the curator inside it. Once Yeha was the capital of Tigrai and according to local tradition the Ark of the Covenant was kept here for some time before being taken to Axum. The ruins of a very large palace, even older than the temple have recently been discovered and are now being excavated. When we left here we returned to the main road and reached our modern hotel on Axum as darkness fell.

Over supper that night we realised we had not seen a single ordinary motor car for the whole of that day. There had been one or two aged buses and lorries. However we had seen another motorised vehicle with which we were to become very well acquainted during the rest of our time on the country. This was the taxi which was to be found on great numbers in every town we went to. It was a three wheeled Chinese machine painted a deep blue. Instead of glass the windows were filled with old sacking to protect the passengers from the dust and the heat of the sun. The driver had plastic instead of glass for the windscreen. Four or even more passengers were pushed into each of these tiny fragile looking vehicles. To judge by the number of these taxis they must have been very cheap to mto buy, run or hire and in all built up areas they wer by far the biggest form of passenger transport.

We were told that the lady who had come by taxi was still not recovered and would be flying home the next day. The general feeling was that her illness was caused by taking her anti Malerial pills long before meals instead of with or after food as instructed. Needless to say we were all very careful about this for the rest of our journey.

Axum is a remarkable city which was for a long time the capital of the whole area and there are a considerable number of remains to be seen.

A standing stele.

The great fallen stele.

We went first to see remarkable tall standing stones called the stele of which there are over forty in a small area. The largest of them lies shattered on the ground where it fell probably during the course of its erection. This would have been 33 m high and weighs some 500 tons. It is said to be the largest single stone ever to have been excavated anywhere in the world. There is an underground tunnel below this containing five burial chambers. However many of the stele are still standing. The largest of these, 26 m high was broken into three for transportation and taken to Rhome by Mussolini and only returned in 2005. These huge stones came from a quarry some four kilometres away and were probably pulled here by elephants.

The excellent little Axum museum is also located in the same area. This holds many fine exhibits including ancient rock tablets with writings carved on them in many different languages, household artefacts and a seven hundred year old bible written in Galez, all of which combine to give an idea of how advanced the city was.

We spent a long time exploring this area before crossing the road to visit a group of churches. The oldest of these was built over an old pagan shrine is closed to women and contains some fine paintings. This church of St. Mary of Zion is a 13th century building constructed when the original 4th century church was pulled down. When we went there we left the ladies in the huge modern church opposite built by Haile Selassie in the 1960's so that all could worship together regardless of sex. This modern church does itself contain some old illustrated books and musical instruments. One of the books was so heavy it required two attendants to show it to us open.I was worried that one of the men did not know how to hold it properly and great strain was being put on the binding.

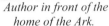

Author in front of the home of the Ark.

A magnificent Jacaranda tree in purple bloom.

We took lunch at another hotel before driving on to see some more of the many sights in the town. He first was a large pond or small reservoir known for some reason as the Bath of the Queen of Sheba. It was larger than an Olympic size swimming pool. We then stopped to see a small pillar inscribed in three languages, Sabaean, Geez and Greek. We were then driven up a steep track to see two large underground tombs of early kings. .Outside these there were several carpets laid out on the ground covered with tourist tat. When we drove back downhill we were raced down by two children one of whom, a girl, of about twelve years, was one of the most remarkable child athletes O have ever seen. Though running barefoot through the rough fields beside the track and having to hurdle many stone walls she easily beat us down and we were not crawling. I hope she is discovered and trained by a suitable person for she could well become a top Olympic athlete.

Our next stop was at the ruins of an old palace containing over fifty rooms which is known as Queen of Sheba's Palace. Some way beyond that was the quarry from where the stones for the stelae had been extracted.   There is still one unfinished stele lying there and another stone with the carving of a large lion etched on it. When we returned to Axum several of us were dropped off so we could explore some of the local shops which were the more interesting for not being aimed at tourists.

The next morning we made a forty minute flight to Lalibela. Once again there was very tight security and during our waiting time I was called back to the security area to open my case. I do not know what they were looking for since they completely ignored the bags containing my spare batteries and any other electrical appliances and just rummaged through my clothing before pronouncing themselves satisfied. When I asked our guide why we took a flight for such a short distance he replied that if we had driven it it would have taken us over fifteen hours driving time such wasthe state of the roads.

Lalibela airport was right out on the country some forty kilometres from the town itself. The drive was through lovely mountain countryside. We had been booked into the Mountain View Hotel which we had been looking forward to because of its name but this had been changed to the Maribela Hotel for some reason. Luckily the mountain views from this hotel were superb and we were all very happy at the change.

Views from my hotel balcony, Lalibela.

After lunch, with a superb soup, we set out to see the Northern group of the rock hewn churches for which Lalibela is famous, all of which are still in use. We had to wait for quite a tome to enter the first of these since it was being used for a wedding. With the exception of one all lie close together and a few of them are now protected by a modern plastic roof mounted on poles. We had to shed our shoes to enter and we had a shoe guardian to look after them while we were inside and to move them to the way out if there was a different exit. He also always found somewhere for me to sit when we had to don them again and helped me which was a relief since my feet had swelled with heat and even with the aid of a shoehorn I was carrying it was a real struggle and shoes were essential for walking around outside for, as a guide book says, "The steps are uneven and walking around can require a little agility".

Medhane Alem church. Lalibela.   *Wedding party leaving Medhane Alem.*

When the wedding party had left we went into Medhane Alem church which was the largest rock hewn church in the world, standing 11.5 m. high and with an area of around 800 m sq. The wall thickness is over 2m. There are over 30 pillars on the inside and the same number on the outside. There is a wide path all round it outside separating it from the cliff from which it had been carved. There are no frescos here but at one point several human sized cavities have been carved which are believed to have been graves. The very uneven floor is covered by a carpet.

When we left this church we walked through a short tunnel in the cliff and emerged into a courtyard where there were three more smaller churches. To reach them we walked past the baptismal pool which I would not have liked to be baptised in since the surface was covered with green algae.

The oldest of these churches is the Biet Maryam which is supposed to have been the first of the churches built in Lalibela. It was considerably more elaborate than the Medhane Alem. There were quite a number of rather worn frescos dating from the twelfth and thirteenth centuries as well as patterns painted on the ceiling. There were also many carvings on the walls and the pillars. The floor was covered not with carpets, but with rugs which were both attractive and rather dangerous since the edges were frequently crumpled up and we had to be very careful not to trip.

Baptismal Pool.

Ceiling of Biet Maryam church.

While we were in there we were given a talk by the priest about the church and its history which was translated to us by our guide. Several other churches had very uneven steps leasing to their entrances but I am glad to say that I managed to enter them all. We then went to visit the church of ST. George which lies at a considerable distance from the rest of the group and down the hill. This is particularly interesting to see from the outside since you look down upon it from above and see the large cross carved on the roof which is level with the ground all around it, and you can also see clearly the narrow path all around it separating it from the rock out of which it has been carved.

After seeing the churches we went to a coffee house, with a musician who played for us for the long time while the coffee was being prepared in the traditional way. When we returned to our hotel we found there was no electricity for there was a power cut over much of the town. Luckily this did not last long. I went out for a short walk and went into a small bookshop not far from the hotel where I found the shop keeper had done a degree in Geology and IT and was now was working for a PHD. When he obtained this he intended to sell the shop and write books.

St. George's church, Lalibela.

The next morning our itinerary gave us the choice for the morning of a walk taking five to six hours from the hotel, at a height of about 2.600 m up to a mountain at about 4,000 m. Enquiries elicited the fact that the estimated time was for the return journey and not the single. Even so I was not the only person who decided to take the alternative which was now to be to take our coach up a very new track to an area only twenty minutes walk from the same church. The new track proved to be very rough and although we started much later than the walkers it still took us about an hour to reach the large flat area at the top. On the way up we had to stop we had to stop to pick up one of our walkers who had been overcome by the altitude, luckily not far from our track. We did not have to wait long for the others and set out to see the church. The path was very rough and uneven and looked still worse further ahead so several of us gave up and returned to where the coach was parked. Shortly after another member of our party returned having been overcome by vertigo and in the end only three of our group reached the church itself and those who did said it had not been worth that last section of the trek except for the magnificent views which were themselves little better than those we had at the parking place. There was one other coach parked before ours and when the occupants returned they proved to be Germans who gave a lift down to one of us. There were also a few huts and a couple of houses around. Some donkeys and ponies were also tied up for rest and to feed and these proved to have been ridden up by other tourists led by several natives on foot. Some carpets were laid out covered by tourist memorabilia. I had quite an interesting time walking about and talking to some of the locals who were there including a group of three young men who were attending different universities for their studies.

Stopping place at 4,000 m

With university students at 4,000 m.

On the return down all of us boarded the coach although we were offered the chance to walk. We had a pizza lunch at the hotel and although pizzas are not normally my favourite dish I enjoyed the Ethiopian version. After lunch we visited the Southern group f rock churches. We had the same shoe minder and he was relieved to see I had chosen to wear sandals with which we had no trouble in putting on again. The track round these churches was once again very rough and some of the church entrances not easy but the visits were well worthwhile.

A church entrance, lalibela. 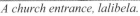 *A church fresco, Lalibela.*

The next day, Saturday, we were due to have a morning flight to Gondar but before we left for the airport we heard that the flight was to be delayed by three hours due to some military air displays at Addis Ababa. However the time was not wasted since we were taken to the weekly open air market in Lalibela. This proved to be the largest open air market I had ever seen. It was selling cattle, sheep, goats, chickens, a certain amount of clothing, as well as lots of produce such as honey, hops, onions and other vegetables but surprisingly no fruit. Nor was there anything for the tourist which was not surprising since we were the only foreigners there. We spent a good time there before moving to the first hotel to be built in Lalibela for coffee. It must once have been a good place to stay but had by now descended to a budget or backpacker residence.

Lalibela open air market.

When we reached the airport we had to pass through the usual Ebola check and then had a very long wait for our plane since although it had originally been scheduled to fly directly to us from Addis Ababa it now had to drive first to Meteke to take some other passengers there before coming on to us. We finally reached Gondar in the late afternoon and set out on a five hour drive to the Simien Mountain Lodge hotel in the Simien Mountains National Park. This was so late that we had to drive direct without any stops but were told we would make all our missed visits on our return journey to Gondar in two days time. It was a lovely journey through hilly scenery. As darkness was falling we were delayed for a time having to pass through a procession of over a hundred three wheel taxis accompanied by many pedestrians going to a town where the next day they would be celebrating the laying of the foundation stone of a new university. It was completely dark by the time we reached the locked gates to the National ark for they were always shut at nightfall. Before they were unlocked for us we took on board two armed soldiers and a park guide. These were to stay with us for the whole of our visit to the area. We were never able to discover if the armed men were there to protect us from wild animals or possible terrorists since we were near the borders of Eritrea. We finally reached the Simien Mountain Lodge, the highest hotel in Africa at nearly 3,300 metres. It was similar to the Gheralta Lodge except that the round thatched huts only held one room each and were all situated on the fairly steep hillside well above the main buildings. Since the paths were very rough and lighting was nearly nonexistent I was very glad I had taken a torch with me. I also found the climb to my room was made more difficult by lack of breath due to the altitude. As at the Gheralta Lodge we were invited to a drink of honey wine before supper, though the taste was very different.

The next day the weather was fine and sunny as we started out in the coach, but it soon clouded over and became cooler though it remained dry with some sunny periods.

Simien Mountain Lodge, Hotel from my room.

The National Park proved to be in a marvellous mountain position with wonderful views across the Simien Mountains which boast of a dozen peaks of over 4,000 m. We could see right across to Eritrea which added to our belief that this was probably the reason for our armed guards. One of our main objectives was to see the Gelada monkeys. There are believed to be some 7,000 of these remarkable animals in the park and there are often up to 400 individuals in each herd of several families. It is the females who run each family and they chose one male who has all mating rights but if another male appears who seems stronger they dismiss their present leader who however remains in the family acting as a sort of grandfather nanny looking after the youngsters. At night they sleep on steep cliff faces to be safe from predators such as hyenas. How they manage to hang onto the cliff face in their sleep in unknown and none have ever been found to have fallen off. They are not in the least afraid of visiting tourists though they are said to be more wary of locals. How they can tell the difference I do not know.

We drove for several miles up a dusty track before stopping and then walking to the top edge of a cliff where some of them often spend the night. They were up by now and running around the hillside above. Back in the coach later on we came across another group who showed no fear at all of the coach and our driver had to go very carefully for they were in no hurry to get out of the way. When we went on foot again two of the young males who were sparring with each other made use of me as a shield between them and ran very closely round me several times to the great amusement of my companions. At one place on the roadside several locals had laid out a mat with curios on it for sale. How well they ever did I cannot imagine since we only saw one other coach all day as well as one elderly lorry. We took a picnic lunch in the open air and found that a species of large black birds, possibly ravens, also had little fear of humans since if anyone laid down a bit of food beside them it would disappear very quickly indeed.

Simien National Park views.

A Gelada monkey.   *One of our guards.*

On our return to the hotel we were shown a film that had been made about one family of Gelada monkeys. Then after supper we retired quickly to our rooms since we were to have an early start the next day for we were to see various things we had missed due to our very delayed flight to the Simien mountains.

The day started cold and cloudy, however it soon warmed up and the sun emerged as we drove down the bumpy track to the park gates where we dropped our two guards and our park guide and where we reached a better surfaced road. Our first stop was at a village to see them gathering water. We were assured that this was not for drinking they had to walk several miles to collect drinking water from a national supply tap for the authorities were trying to to make fresh water available over the whole country. Nevertheless I saw one boy drinking this water where a cow was walking and vultures were tearing at the carcass of a dead horse. Water aid has still a very long way to go here.

Our next stop was to see several horses being led round in circles to thresh the corn with their hooves. We then visited a school of young children at which we gave a large bag of ball point pens to the head teacher and for which she solemnly wrote out a receipt. We had frequently been besieged by children begging, not for for money or sweets, but for pens. Outside the school was a large notice which read (as in many notices in Ethiopia) in English followed by Arabic "In order to make children not to be migrated, let us help and educate them in their localitie's." I should say that I was often chased by children wanting to try out their English. The most frequent ploy was for them to say, "Tell me the name of a country and I will tell you its capital". Nearly always they got it right. Not far from Gondar we stopped at a village which we had noticed on our way up to the National Park because it had a large Star of David hanging by the roadside. It proved to be a village of Jews who had gone to Israel and then returned home because they found Ethiopia a much happier place in which to live. The whole village was made up of houses turned into little shops all selling, unusual for Ethiopia, lots of trinkets for tourists. I actually succumbed and bought a little statuette of Solomon and Sheba with their baby son.

Jewish village near Gondar

Village water supply.

We spent some time at both of these stops so when we reached Gondar we drove straight to the Three Sisters restaurant for lunch.

Gondar, Three Sisters Restaurant.

This was a remarkable establishment. We were ushered in by two musicians one of whom was one of the sisters. We then found the wooden walls and the ceiling were covered in paintings, some of biblical scenes, one of which was the most unusual pictures of The Last Supper that I have ever seen On top of all this the buffet lunch gave us a large choice of excellent dishes and the meal finished with yet another delicious cup of coffee.

There is a lot to see in Gondar which was once the capital of Ethiopia. Our first visit was to the group of castles in the Royal Compound which was surrounded by high walls. There are the ruins of six castles as well as several other smaller buildings. The most impressive of these is Fasilida's Castle built in the mid seventeenth century and restored recently with the help of UNESCO. During the Second World War the Italian headquarters was established inside the compound and was bombed by the British so that much damage was done but the remaining ruins made the visit very worthwhile. There were only a few other visitors though it was a place that would have attracted many had it been in Western Europe.

Gondar. Castles in the Royal Compound.

Our next trip was to the Bath of Fasilida. This was empty at the time of our visit though we gathered that at the Ethiopian Epiphany it is filled with water from a nearby river so that worshippers can enter th e water to re-enact the baptism of Jesus. It was particularly interesting to see the huge tangled roots of several large Banyan trees which covered some of the outer walls and steps.

Building standing in the Bath of Fasilida.

Banyan tree roots over bath walls.

After that we went to see the 17th century church of Debre Berhan Selassie., probably much restored after a fire caused by lightning in the 18th. Century. This does not look anything special from the outside but inside the waslls and ceiling were covered with paintings the best, I thought, we had seen so far. The ceiling alone has some eighty faces painted on it. It is the only church left in Gondar from this period since the others had all been destroyed in a Sudanese Muslim Dervish invasion in 1888. It, according to legend, had only been saved by a swarm of bees who had attacked and driven away the invaders.

Frescos in Debre Berhan Selassie church in Gondar.

Finally we drove to our hotel a few miles outside Gondar. This hotel, the Mayleko, Lodge was built in the same style as the hotel we had left. However when we arrived we found the water supply had been cut off and would not be restored for several days. We were given the choice of returning to an otherwise less goo hotel back in Gondar but on being assured that each room would be given a water container holding several gallons of cold but drinkable fresh water we decided to stay since it would have taken half an hour to drive back and we would have to drive out this way the next day, for otherwise the place seemed very pleasant and indeed we had an excellent dinner plus a free glass of a good wine.

Tuesday proved to be a marvellous day. We were due to take a boat trip on Lake Tana the source of the Blue Nile. One of our party decided not to take the boat trip and instead took a taxi to our next destination a town called Bahir Dar on the other side of the lake. The rest of us took the coach on an awful track, some of it still being made up, to Gorgora an the northern shore of the lake. Here we visited a 17th century monastery with its round thatched church of Debre Sina Maryam decorated with wonderful frescos. This was the first round and first thatched church we had visited in Ethiopia and that visit by itself would have made the whole trip worthwhile.

Gorgora, church of Debre Sina Maryam.& a fresco of the Massacre of the Innocents.

their face visible while the full faced people are the good. When we had seen the church we walked through the graveyard to the boatyard where a motorised boat had been reserved for us. The boat had a crew of two one to work the engine and steer the vessel and the other, a woman, to bring us drinks and prepare our picnic lunch, which we took after a couple of hours sailing on what looked almost like open sea, such is the size of the lake. The weather was excellent and it was good to relax after several strenuous days.

Shortly after lunch we stopped at an island where we visited another round church. It had obviously once been thatched but now sported a corrugated iron roof. This was the church of Nrga Sillasse and was an 18th century building and again was decorated inside with many more fine frescos.

Church of Nrga Sillasse on a lake Tana island with frescos.

Another few hours sailing brought us to a peninsula where there is yet another round church called Abunc Beter Maryam. To see this church we had to walk uphill on a track through a coffee forest for about a quarter of an hour. This 19th century church was thatched and also fully decorated with murals, though I felt that these more modern pictures lacked a certain amount of the naïve charm of the earlier churches.

Cxhurch of Abune Beter Maryam with fresco.

Another hour's sailing brought us to Bahir Dar, where we were to spend the next two nights. This proved to be a large lakeside town with a mixture of modern urban buildings, rural markets and housing. We were also to see a number of ordinary cars as well as the usual lorries and three wheeled taxis. We were met by our coach which had driven round the lake and taken to to our hotel, the Kuriftu Resort and Spa. This was in a lovely lakeside position and sported an attractive swimming pool as well as a fine large garden. The rooms were spacious though not as pleasant as those in the mountain lodges. I was glad there were no mosquitoes in my room for the mosquito netting over my bed had several large holes in it. However the netting itself was a reminder that for the first time on our trip the height was below 2,000 m and we were now in an area where Malaria could be contracted, though it was not usually found until the rainy season later in the year. There was a power cut shortly after our arrival but luckily power was restored before dinner time since some of the uneven paths from our rooms would have been very dark by the time we had finished.

The next day we started off driving to the Blue Nile Falls. Immediately after leaving Bahir Dar the road turned into a rough track. Our first stop was by a huge rubbish dump. The reason for the stop was to see two tall trees. One of these was occupied by a large number of vultures and the other by Storks all of who had found the dump a marvellous feeding place.

Vultures ready for food.   *Maribou Storks ready for food.*

The track continued for some twenty miles through several villages most of which looked very poor. We eventually came to a stop in a village at the end of the track from where we had a short walk to the bank of the Blue Nile and took a ferry over it, then took a footpath for about a mile through the fields which led us out to a hill overlooking the falls. Although it was now the dry season the falls were very impressive and I imagine must have looked magnificent during the rainy period due in about three months.

Ferryover Blue Nile.   *Blue Nile Falls.*

Several of the more energetic members of our group scrambled down to obtain a closer view but several of us stayed above and I spent some time chatting to an old man who lived nearby and was the only othe spectator at the time we were there. The other ferry crossers who lived on this side of the river but had not made their way to the falls.

Old man by the Blue Nile fall

River traffic above the falls.

Village by the ferry.

Harvesting by the Blue Nile.

We drove back to the hotel for lunch and were then driven up the hill above the town to see the entrance to Haile Selassie's palace. Clearly nothing had been done to this building since his death and the gates were firmly locked. However there was a good view of the Blue Nile as it left Lake Tana. We were also able to see, with the aid of binoculars a hippopotamius wallowing in the water. On our way back to the hotel we visited another very large market with a sizeable section devoted to spices, but still nothing for the tourist.

A spice market.

An Ethiopian Taxi.

The next, our final morning we flew back to Addis Ababa and after a drive round the huge old market, which we had not seen before we were taken back to our hotel which had prepared rooms for us in which to rest until the evening when we were taken to a cultural restaurant with dancing until we left for the airport for our midnight flight back to the UK. For the first time we did not have to go through an Ebola check since we were leaving the country.

Chapter Eight

Serbia: A New Country; built from the old Yugoslavia.

Mosaics in the Kiaradorde Mausoleum, Topola.

Jacynth, my wife, and I had in the past made many visits to Yugoslavia before the civil war and had then visited several of the new countries that had risen from the ruins. However I realised I had not visited Serbia since and wished to see its painted churches again as well as the capital, Belgrade, which I had not seen since 1955. So on Tuesday 19th May 2015 I drove to the Sheraton Hotel at Heathrow.

The next morning I timed matters well by arriving at the Air Serbia desk in Terminal 4. Just as it was opening. At security I set off the security alarm and had to take off my shoes and be hand searched. It was only later that I realised that it was the zip on my trousers that had caused the trouble! The flight to Belgrade was comfortable and despite a delayed start we arrived to find sunny weather and a temperature of 32 Celsius. I was met and taken to the hotel Argo and on the way there saw a Belgrade tram with several children hanging onto its back. The hotel itself proved to be fairly basic and by normal Western standards might have gained a two* classification despite the lack of a lift. .and the welcome was very friendly. There was an early muddle when the part of my passport that was photocopied by the hotel proved to be my Iranian Visa, which did have my photo on it, instead of the basic information page. This mistake by them caused much amusement to all. Later in the evening I was collected by my driver and taken to an excellent open air restaurant in a delightful pedestrian only area. Luckily my driver arrived to take me back to the hotel shortly before it started to rain.

I found the sun was shining the next morning when I woke and it remained dry for most of the day. My guide, Peter, came for me and took me to our car which was to be driven by a man whose name sounded something like "Dervish". We went first to see the new cathedral of, St. Sava said to be the second largest orthodox church in the world (The largest is in Moscow) .While it is now open the inside is not yet finished and the walls there will be covered in Carara marble and mosaic copies of famous frescos. We also visited the very crowded little church next door, also named St. Sava, which is usually being used for most services until the main cathedral is completed. This was a typical small Orthodox church whose walls are covered in old frescos.

We were then driven across the Danube by the most recent of several new bridges, supported by one 211 metre high column, to New Belgrade from where we had fine views of the old city and could see how the new cathedral dominated all the buildings around it. New Belgrade is rightly named for when we had visited the city back in 1955 there were no buildings at all on this side of the river. It is an attractive new area with many parks and gardens. I gathered that this was where the upper classes now chose to live.

After a short stop at a cafe with a good view we went back across the river and up to the Kalemegdan fortress. This was the first place that I could remember from my earlier visit so long before which still looked down across the junction of the Danube and the Sava rivers and across to New Belgrade with all its new buildings. The building was undergoing some restoration and there was now one area with several market stall at one of which I made a small purchase and was then presented with a packet of different banknotes from the time inflation of the civil war and one of which was to the value of 500000000000 lira, said to be in the Guinness book of records as the largest figure banknote ever published in the world. The stall holder told Peter that she had given me this since I would be bound to be interested in it since I looked so Aristocratic!

St. Sava Cathedral.   *Little church of St. Sava.*

Kalemegdan Fortress.

We spent some time exploring the castle before walking to the nearby pedestrian area. Just opposite from this was what Peter told me was the oldest church in Belgrade. I then recognised it as being the first Orthodox church that I had ever visited back in 1955. Inside is a huge iconostasis and a large number of frescos. Unfortunately photography was not allowed inside and there were not even any postcards for sale. Nor could I find a position where I was able to find a position from which I could take an external photograph all of which was most frustrating.

I was delivered back to the hotel at lunch time and in the afternoon I took quite a long walk around the neighbourhood with its parks before being picked up in the evening and driven to a floating restaurant on the banks of the Danube where I had an excellent supper before being driven back to the Argo.

Belgrade park.   *Danube floating restaurant.*

The next morning the TV in the hotel restaurant at breakfast showed pictures of Palmyra which had just fallen to ISIS in the war in Syria.

The weather outside the hotel was raining which was to be intermittent for the whole of the day. Peter arrived with a large bag of chocolates as a gift to me which was a pleasant surprise. There was also a new driver called Deki who was to be my driver for the whole of the rest of my holiday. Peter was not to be with us after this day's trip but I was to find Deki spoke reasonable English and other guides had been arranged for future visits.

We drove first to the Krusedol Monastery on the slopes of the Fruska Gora mountain. Here we were lucky for it had just stopped raining but the weather had put off other visitors and Peter had to find a monk with a key. He had to leave shortly and we were joined by a professor who was responsible for restoring the fine frescos and paintings who told me to take some photos of the frescos before any monks reappeared for photography was officially forbidden.

Krusedol Monastery.

161

Peter told me that in fine weather he had often to wait for half an hour to enter because of the size of the tour groups so that we had in fact been lucky with the damp conditions.

The rain started again as we drove on to Novi Sad but once again we were lucky for it stopped just as we reached the city. This was a place that I had never visited before, but had heard enough about it to look forward to seeing it. The whole of the central area was pedestrianised and was very full when we started walking since a local TV company was holding an entertainment there but once we had passed this section the streets were nearly empty so we were able to view the attractive 19th, century buildings in comfort and to visit an attractive church with no one else inside

Novi Sad.

When we met our car again we drove back across the Danube to the fortress on the other side from we had a good view back over the city. Here we walked round together with a large party of school children. In the fortress is a large clock tower where, confusingly, the large arrow hand marks the hours and the small the minutes.

From the fortress we drove a few miles to the historic little town Sremski Karlovci which my guide book says is one of the most attractive towns in the whole country Unfortunately we could not see it at its best because of the misty drizzle but we visited the cathedral before going to a small wine making place where as well as tasting several excellent wines we also visited the owner's small museum for a talk on honey making which was his other occupation.

On out return to Belgrade I was shown a good restaurant near my hotel where I had an excellent supper backed up by another glass of a fine red wine.

View of Novi Sad from across the Danube.   *Inside the winery museum.*

The next day, Saturday, Deki arrived to drive me away from Belgrade bringing with him a gift of fresh strawberries from his own garden. We started off in rain but. soon patches of blue sky appeared and we began to hope for better things. It was a false hope and by the time we reached our first stop, the remains of a huge Roman fortress at Viminacium, there was a thunderstorm raging. Much of the castle still remains to be excavated but, luckily, several, sections which have been dug up are under cover. While we were waiting for our English speaking guide in the reception area Deki showed me some pictures of his four year old son who has started martial arts and has already won some competitions. The firs room we visited was a complex with some underground tombs with frescos. Much bending was needed to see these and it was difficult to hear what the guide was saying due to the noise of the rain on the roof. Luckily by the time we left here the downpour had stopped. Deki then drove us to the next building, a museum built like a Roman villa. This had not yet been completed but I was shown round the both the opened areas and then the parts where the exhibits were still being arranged which were still not officially open to the public. We were then driven along a very muddy track to a third building housing the remains of several dinosaurs which had been discovered in a nearby coal mine.

Viminacium tombs.

Viminacium museum.   *Dinosaur museum.*

We next drove on to a café with lovely views overlooking the Danube, so wide at this point that it looked almost like the seaside, where we were served with a delicious chicken soup and I discovered a very good Serbian beer. The rain had now stopped and it remained dry for the rest of the day. We were lucky with this for two days later this little town where we had stopped was flooded and quite a number of houses, including our café, had to be evacuated.

After lunch we drove on down the Danube which now narrowed to normal river size with Romania on the opposite bank. At one point we drove past the ruins of a riverside fortress and at another we saw a huge face carved on the cliff on the Romanian side. Our first stop was to see the large Mesolithic archaeological site of Lepenski Vir, dating from over 5,300 BC. There is a very large museum here including some remarkable carved stone heads as well as some of the tools and utensils that were discovered during the excavations as well as the bases of several houses. Part of the museum is in the open air but a large area is covered. Once again I was shown round by an English speaking guide.

Inside Mesolithic hut.

Carved face across Danube in Romania.

The next stop was at a small hilltop gallery, museum and café with marvellous views of the Danube as well as many sculptures for sale made by the owner out of many different natural materials. After this we drove to our four star hotel at Kladovo with excellent Danube views and where Deki also stayed and ate supper with me.

Café museum with Danube view.

Danube & Romania view from Kladovo room.

That night I was woken at 2.am by a thunderstorm and torrential rain and though I soon got to sleep I was woken again only two hours later by the same weather conditions. Luckily the rain had stopped when we left Zlatibor at nine though it was still very cloudy and looked threatening for most of the day. The main road was nearly empty of traffic and we made very good time to the old Roman palace of the Emperor Galerius Valerian Maximus, who had been born a commoner and was the last Roman Emperor and was the final Emperor to have been proclaimed a god. We were the only visitors at the site, though it was a Sunday a day in which most Serbian sites are open. An excellent English speaking guide was waiting for us who gave me a fine tour around this large and interesting place. At the end we met the curator who told us that the finds from the site were on show in a local museum only fifteen minutes drive away and that he would lead us there and would open it up for us for it, unlike the site, was closed on Sundays. When we arrived he gave us, with free entry, a superb tour round the fine museum which, he told us, had been voted the best museum in Serbia the previous year.

Roman Palace of Emperor Galerius Valerian Maximus.

The highest value Yugosloav bank note ever produced as legal currency during the civil war inflation.

Chapter Nine

An Island Revisited After Over Forty Years.

Monreale Cathedral.

In September 2015 I set out to visit Sicily an island of which I had fond memories of visits from over forty years before once with Jacynth, my wife, and on another occasion with Elinor, my daughter, as well. I had no idea as to how much I would find it changed, though I expected to find more tourists. The flight to Catania was punctual and a group of nine of us were met at the airport by Massimo who was to be our guide, and when we arrived at our hotel by another pair who arrived later by a different flight. Our hotel was comfortable and situated in a large square with views over to Mount Etna. As usual I found myself the eldest of the group though this was the first time I had travelled in a group where I was the only single person present. Luckily they were all very friendly and I was never allowed to feel alone.

After lunch we set out by coach to a nearby village on the coast with tall stones rising from the sea which legend says were thrown there by Cyclops but which, we were told, did in fact predate Etna the origin of the legend.

Village near Catania.

As we drove back to Catania the sun disappeared and after we had left the coach and were inspecting the ruins of the Roman Amphitheatre, not very spectacular since the greater part of it had been built over by the modern city, the heavens suddenly opened. Luckily we were ushered into the shelter of the lobby of the museum by the guard there even though the building was officially closed and, since the cloudburst only lasted for about quarter of an hour, we did not need to use the services of the large number of umbrella sellers who had suddenly appeared as the downpour started.

Catania city square in the rain.   *Catania Cathedral.*

As soon as the rain stopped we waded through the flooded street to see the cathedral before taking our coach back to the hotel. Since, except for breakfast meals were not included in the cost I set out to find somewhere to eat and near the hotel found a small restaurant and when I went in to it found two members of our group already there so joined them for an excellent supper.

The next day we left for Syracuse at 8am after a good buffet breakfast. Massimo wanted to leave early to beat the large number of groups expected, especially as it was sunny and hot. He was successful in this for as we left the fine classical ruins the crowds were starting to pour in, but we had not been inconvenienced by the numbers. I was particularly interested to see, once again, the impressive Greek Theatre, one of the finest remaining from the classical world and the Roman amphitheatre as well as several other classical remains including the cave, named 'Ear of Dionysus' from where, according to legend, the Syracuseans had been able to listen to what their Greek prisoners working in the salt mines below were saying, and make sure that they were not plotting to escape.

Syracuse Greek Theatre.   *Syracuse 'Ear of Dionysus*   *Syracuse waterfall in cliff.*

After leaving the Archaeological Park we were driven to the present day city. Here we had to park our coach some way from Ortygia the main baroque centre and take an attractive, walk to reach the central square. The first place we came to was the Roman Temple of Apollo. This impressive ruin had been built a considerable distance from the other classical remains which we had seen in the Archaeological Park. We next walked up the hill to reach the nineteenth century main square where we saw a bride in her wedding dress sitting in an open carriage being pulled by a horse. Instead of the normal wedding photographer there was a little drone, with a camera attached flying along beside it. From the square we carried on downhill until we reached an old freshwater pond with large papyrus plants growing in it. This pool was only separated from the saltwater of the sea by a narrow raised road. So it was surprising that it had not been contaminated by salt over the course of centuries. We were given free time to explore from the square and several of us managed to find a pleasant small café in which to refresh ourselves with lunch before leaving for our afternoon visits. Some of us also visited the shops but I did not buy anything.

Syracuse. Temple of Apollo.   *Syracuse. Main Square and wedding.*

We now travelled to Ragusa. We had been going to visit Modica on the way but we were stopped by the police from turning to the town because the road into it was blocked by a bad fire. As a result we had to drive a longer way round which took us over what we were told was at 500 m the highest viaduct in Europe. Unfortunately we were not able to stop ,to take photos of Modica from this viewpoint because of the traffic, but did find a place a little further on to get some more distant views of the town. As a result of the diversion we approached Ragusa, the most southerly town in Sicily, from above and had a steep drive down into the old part of the town, built in 1693, after an earthquake, in the baroque style with its fine Church of St. George before walking up to the 18th.century cathedral in the newer part of the town.

View of Modica from above.   *Ragusa. Church of St. George.*   *Ragusa Cathedral.*

On our arrival back at the hotel I went with two other members of our group to the same restaurant that I had found the previous day where our meal was, they told me, much better than they had eaten the previous evening. Outside our hotel there seemed to be a permanent and very persistent beggar woman with her baby. We decided afterwards that she was quite probably one of the refugees who had fled to Europe from Syria or Libya many of whom had landed in Sicily though we saw few of them on the rest of our trip.

We left Catania the next morning on what proved to be a very hot and humid day. It was to be a long day and we had a comfort stop on the motorway before reaching Agrigento which was to be our first visit. Here, possibly because it was a Sunday, we encountered crowds of visitors. We parked in the coach park and then took the path to the top of the so called 'Valley of the Temples. Why it is called a valley I do not know for it is in fact a ridge gradually running down from a high point. At the top there is the 5 century B.C. Temple of Hera We then walked down by the ruins of what would have been shops to the, also 5th,century B.C. Temple of Concorde which is one of the best preserved Doric temples in the world, and which had for a short time been used as a Christian church. In front of it was a modern metal statue of the fallen Icarus lying on the ground. Next was the oldest, at 6th.century B.C. Temple of Heracles. of which only the columns remain. Then to the completely unreconstructed fragments the Temple of Olympian Zeus which at 100 m long is possibly the largest classical temple ever built. Finally we saw the four surviving columns of the Temple of Castor and Pollex. All in all it is one of the finest collection of classical remains I have ever seen. Before leaving we had a good lunch, with some excellent draft beer at a pre-booked café table. We were not able to visit the town of Agrigento itself since traffic is forbidden to enter its steep and narrow streets. I have still not seen the town since on my previous visit it had been closed by a recent earthquake.

Agrigento. Temple of Hera.   *Agrigento. Temple of Concorde.*

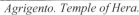

We now had a drive to Selinunte, another classical site holding the ruins of what was once one of the largest and richest cities in the world with the remains of several large temples. While we were walking to see Temple C on the Acropolis with a very fine position overlooking the beach at which the allied forces had landed during the second World War a middle aged lady, with, one of the groups of visitors, suddenly rushed up to me calling me by name. I did not recognise her at all at first which was not really surprising for I had last seen her over thirty years before as a thirteen year old child I had been teaching. I had evidently not changed as much as she had over the years. She was only the third ex pupil of mine I can remember having met on one of my trips abroad. The finest of the temples remaining was Temple E another Doric temple and considered on of the best examples remaining in Italy though not quite as well preserved as the Temple of Concorde in Agrigento. Selinunte was an attractive as well as an interesting place, though I have not discovered why this is the only place in which each of the temples has just been called by a letter and not by a name.

Selinunte. Temple E.   *Selinunte beach.*   *Selinunte. Temple C*
on Acropolis

Another hour's driving took us to the Baglio Oneto hotel at Marsala. This 18th.century building was renovated to retain the architectural integrity of its original design with its lovely gardens and views to the sea out over the countryside with its olive groves, Mediterranean flora and vineyards. We all dined, very well, in the hotel open air restaurant since it was some way out of the town and drank the excellent wine from its own vineyards. All in all it was probably the best hotel we stayed in during the whole of our trip for it also boasted very comfortable rooms and a fine swimming pool.

Baglio Oneto hotel.

The next morning we were delayed starting since a faulty computer had charged several of us, not me, for two nights instead of one and it took Massimo some time to get the matter settled correctly.

Our first stop, not long after leaving the hotel was at some salt pans and a windmill as we were approaching Trapani. The windmill was used to drain the water from the pans to allow the salt to dry out so it could be loaded into lorries to be taken away and put to use. Shortly after leaving the pans we stopped at a red traffic light where we were accosted by an apparent migrant trying to raise contributions. I fear he did not receive anything from us nor as far as we could see did he have greater success from other vehicles that he approached.

Erice was approached by a very steep and windy road for it is perched on the top of a high hill. We had to park near the entrance gate for only local residents were allowed to take their vehicles into the town itself which meant that the steep cobbled streets were almost as safe as a pedestrianised zone. It was a very attractive little place and well worth the walk up to the top of the town both for the views and the architecture. It was almost empty when we arrived for despite our delayed start we were well ahead of the tourist groups who came on a day trip from Palermo. Indeed they were just arriving in fleets of coaches, when we were leaving.

Erice with its view.

We were told that the previous day the road up to Erice had been closed for a motor race. That brought back memories of my last visit here so many years before when we had met several vehicles practising for a race. I had forgotten quite how steep and windy the road was, surpassing even the road up the cliff face from Kotor to Cetigne in Montenegro, and the thought of a race here was almost unbelievable. The heavy cloud with which we had started the day began to clear and it became very hot and sticky so the stop at a café to sample a local delicacy with some coffee was more than welcome before our drive down to sea level and on towards Palermo.

Our next stop was at Monreale on a hill outside Palermo. This time we had to park the coach well down from the magnificent cathedral and had to climb a flight of many steps to a restaurant which was not far from the plateau upon which the cathedral and town stood. Here we stopped, since the cathedral was closed for the lunch time siesta, had an excellent lunch and were able to admire the fine, if somewhat misty, views. After lunch we walked around the attractive town and looked at the many shops, aimed at the large number of visitors, until the cathedral opened again.

Despite the crowds we were still able to get a good view of the magnificent mosaics. These included one of Thomas a Becket which was extraordinary since he had only been murdered in Canterbury Cathedral a dozen years before Monreale Cathedral itself was completed. I was, unfortunately, unable to find a position from which I was able to photograph St. Thomas himself. The cathedral is definitely one of the greatest achievements of Norman-Arabic art, and we spent a long time viewing the interior as well as the fine cloisters.(See the title page of this Chapter).

Monreale Cathedral and cloisters.

Our hotel in Palermo, an art nouveau style of building with a small garden in front, was well positioned and very comfortable though there was a considerable amount of traffic noise. After our arrival I was able to take a walk and was lucky to find an open air restaurant whose white house wine, from Messina, proved to be as fine as any I have ever tasted.

The next day started very cloudy and humid and it remained very hot all day with occasional sunshine later and a couple of sharp but short showers in the afternoon. We went first to see the Norman Palace with its glorious church the Capella Palatina. This, like Monreale is full of wonderful golden mosaics. Everyone had to be respectably dressed to enter here and all women had to have their shoulders covered. We were lucky in the time of our visit for we were both preceded and followed by huge groups but the building was not too crowded at the time we were there.

Palermo. The Capella Palatina.

After leaving the palace we walked to the 12th century cathedral, built on the site of a Roman Christian basilica .which had later become a mosque. This should have been a short walk but at one point restoration of the Porte Nuova with its arch over the road had just been completed and the scaffolding was being removed so we had to make a very long diversion. Due to many restorations and alterations not much remains of the original cathedral but it is still a fine building though it lacks the exciting mosaics of Monreale and the Capella Palatina.

Palermo Cathedral.

After leaving the cathedral we walked uphill through a very crowded food street market in the Arab quarter of the old city. In the middle of this we visited the extraordinary baroque church of Chiesa del Gesu. For some reason, possibly because one can only reach it on foot, there were no other groups here at all.

Palermo. Church of Chiesa del Gesu.

After reaching the top of the market we boarded our coach again for further touring. We passed the Piazza Marina Park and stopped to see what is claimed to be the largest Magnolia tree in Europe and possibly in the world. The circumference is said to be over 50 feet and still growing. We had to drive past San Cataldo with its distinctive three red domes since it was shut, possibly for restoration, so we were unable to see the inside. Near the harbour itself outside one of the Palazzos stands a large wooden chariot holding a statue of the virgin which, once a year, is pulled through the streets of the city. Those of us who wished to do further exploration by ourselves were dropped off near the opera house. I found a pleasant café nearby where I had lunch before I started walking. I walked round the Fontana Pretoria, originally built in the 16th century for a Florentine garden and later transferred here. It is sometimes called the Fountain of Shame for the large number of nude statues. I then went to the nearby opera house for I had discovered there was to be an English speaking tour of the interior. This has a stage so large that in the 1970s a real elephant and horses appeared on it in a performance of Aida. Our small group was lucky for we were able to watch, from the royal box, part of a rehearsal, though none of us was able to recognise what the actual opera was.

Palermo. Magnolia.   *Palermo. Fontana Pretoria.*   *Palermo. Statue of Virgin Mary*

174

Palermo. Opera House.   *Palermo. Fountain.*   *Quatro Venti Crossroads.*

I then walked back alomg the main street to the hotel, stopping frequently to look at the shops. At one point I sheltered from a shower in a café where I ate one of the most delicious ice creams I have ever tasted. It was interesting to see how, as in Catania, a large number of umbrella sellers once again suddenly appeared with the rain. Later in the evening I went to the same restaurant I had visited the previous night. The house wine was different this time and though good not up to the standard of the previous evening.

The next day we were to have a long drive to Taormina with a stop at the 3rd -4th century Roman Villa del Casale with its famous mosaics. The weather forecast was ominous with warnings of a big storm. We set off in the dry on the coastal motorway but shortly after it turned inland the road was closed by the police because of the collapse of a bridge. We started along the narrow mountain deviation but at one point at one turning our driver thought there would be a shorter route so enquired of this from the police at the junction but was advised that though that way was still open in view of the coming storm he would be strongly advised to take the signposted route or we could well be trapped. We took the police advice. The predicted storm did not actually hit until shortly after we had rejoined the motorway and were approaching the site of the villa at Piazza Armerina By the time we reached the car park the rain was starting to increase. Luckily we all had some protective clothing and umbrellas available for while we were visiting the rainfall steadily increased to torrential proportions. While all the wonderful mosaics were under cover there were several areas that had to be approached from outside and such was the strength of the rain that despite our rain protections we were all soaked by the time we reached our coach again. Despite the wet it was well worth the visit for the classical mosaics are some of the finest in the world. I must admit that I might have been more worried had I realised that the villa had only been discovered in the 19th century after being buried in mud from a flood in the 12th century. The six hours rainfall we had that day gave a downfall more than was normally averaged in three months.

Mosaics from Villa Romana del Casale at Piazza Armerina.

Our drive to Taormina from Piazza Armerina must have been terrible for our driver since water was falling in bucketfulls from the sides of the roads which were flooded quite deeply in places. We did not make the scheduled stop for lunch since that would have meant a walk through flooded roads and instead stopped where we could drive up to the front door. Luckily the rain eased a little as we reached our hotel at Taormina but even so all of us stayed in the hotel for supper. The meal was good and the hotel was comfortable which was just as well since, though within walking distance from the centre of the town it was quite an uphill pull.

Thursday was to be our last full day and mercifully it was dry all day with occasional sunny periods. We started by driving to Mount Etna and as far up it as the road went. Here there were several small shops and one of the many small craters round which we were able to walk. Much of the time the top of the mountain was swathed in cloud or mist but there were several occasion on which the clouds cleared and we were able briefly to see the summit In one of the shops I purchased a small elephant carved out of the local stone and I also bought a very crude lava face carved by a man in the open who was sculpting images from small pieces of larva which he was picking up at the site.

Up Mount Etna..

We spent well over an hour up on the mountain before being driven back to the centre of Taormina where we were dropped to explore before meeting in a small restaurant for lunch. Although I had been expecting a lot of tourists here I was unprepared for the huge number filling the streets so fully that at times it was almost impossible to make a way between them.

The lunch was to be our final get together since our guide was leaving after it for Catania to meet a new group, leaving us free for the afternoon.

Our final lunch.

I spent quite a long time after lunch exploring the town which was still attractive despite the large number of tourists. There is a marvellous view from the theatre, the second largest in Sicily even when, as on this occasion, the summit of Etna itself was obscured by cloud.

Taormina Greek Theatre.

Taomina town centre.

Taomina view from hotel.

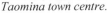

I walked back to the hotel for a short siesta before a final walk up to the town for a last meal. Early next morning we were picked up and driven to Catania Airport for our flight back to the UK to end an enjoyable and most interesting tour despite the number of tourists and the mixed weather.

Printed in the United States
By Bookmasters